FIVE SWEDISH POETS

Some other books from Norvik Press

Hjalmar Söderberg: *Short stories* (translated by Carl Lofmark)

Annegret Heitmann (ed.): *No Man's Land. An Anthology of Modern Danish Women's Literature*

P C Jersild: *A Living Soul* (translated by Rika Lesser)

Sara Lidman: *Naboth's Stone* (translated by Joan Tate)

Selma Lagerlöf: *The Löwensköld Ring* (translated by Linda Schenck)

Villy Sørensen: *Harmless Tales* (translated by Paula Hostrup-Jessen)

Camilla Collett: *The District Governor's Daughters* (translated by Kirsten Seaver)

Jens Bjørneboe: *The Sharks* (translated by Esther Greenleaf Mürer)

Jørgen-Frantz Jacobsen: *Barbara* (translated by George Johnston)

Janet Garton & Henning Sehmsdorf (eds. and trans.): *New Norwegian Plays* (by Peder W.Cappelen, Edvard Hoem, Cecilie Løveid and Bjørg Vik)

Gunilla Anderman (ed.): *New Swedish Plays* (by Ingmar Bergman, Stig Larsson, Lars Norén and Agneta Pleijel)

Kjell Askildsen: *A Sudden Liberating Thought* (translated by Sverre Lyngstad)

Svend Åge Madsen: *Days with Diam* (translated by W. Glyn Jones)

Christopher Moseley (ed.): *From Baltic Shores*

Janet Garton (ed.): *Contemporary Norwegian Women's Writing*

Fredrika Bremer: *The Colonel's Family* (translated by Sarah Death)

Hans Christian Andersen (ed.): *New Danish Plays* (by Sven Holm, Kaj Nissen, Astrid Saalbach and Jess Ørnsbo)

Suzanne Brøgger: *A Fighting Pig's Too Tough to Eat* (translated by Marina Allemano)

Kerstin Ekman: *Witches' Rings* (translated by Linda Schenck)

Gunnar Ekelöf: *Modus Vivendi* (edited and translated by Erik Thygesen)

The logo of Norvik Press is based on a drawing by Egil Bakka (University of Bergen) of a Viking ornament in gold, paper thin, with impressed figures (size 16x21mm). It was found in 1897 at Hauge, Klepp, Rogaland, and is now in the collection of the Historisk museum, University of Bergen (inv.no. 5392). It depicts a love scene, possibly (according to Magnus Olsen) between the fertility god Freyr and the maiden Gerðr; the large penannular brooch of the man's cloak dates the work as being most likely 10th century.

Cover illustration: Eva Forsberg.

FIVE SWEDISH POETS

Kjell Espmark
Lennart Sjögren
Eva Ström
Staffan Söderblom
Werner Aspenström

Selected and translated
by

Robin Fulton

Norvik Press
Norwich
1997

A catalogue record for this book is available from the British Library.

ISBN 1-870041-34-8

First published in 1997 by Norvik Press, University of East Anglia, Norwich, NR4 7TJ, England.
Managing Editors: James McFarlane, Janet Garton and Michael Robinson.

Norvik Press was established with financial support from the University of East Anglia, the Danish Ministry for Cultural Affairs, The Norwegian Cultural Department, and the Swedish Institute. Publication of this volume has been aided by a grant from the Swedish Institute.

Printed in Great Britain by Page Bros. (Norwich) Ltd., Norwich, UK.

ACKNOWLEDGEMENTS

Many of the translations gathered in this book have previously appeared in magazines and acknowledgements are due to: *The Edinburgh Review* (Edinburgh), *The Guardian* (London & Manchester), *Inside Sweden* (Stockholm), *The Journal of Contemporary Anglo-Scandinavian Poetry* (Taunton, Somerset), *The Malahat Review* (Victoria, British Columbia), *Modern Poetry in Translation* (London), *Ninth Decade* (London), *Poesie Europe* (Frankfurt-am-Main), *Southfields* (London), *The Times Literary Supplement* (London), and *Trafika* (Prague). 'Archetype' was translated for inclusion in *Outstretched Leaves on his Bamboo Staff — Studies in Honour of Göran Malmkvist* (Stockholm, 1994).

Preface

If poetry translation is a form of vandalization then I have been vandalizing the work of these five poets on and off for many years, in the case of Aspenström and Espmark since the early 1970s and in the case of the other three since the early 1980s. The present gathering complements previous publications without in any way overlapping with them. Oasis Books (London) published a selection of Aspenström poems in 1977 and a selection of his prose in 1981, and then a selection of Espmark poems in 1985. In *Four Swedish Poets* (White Pine Press, Fredonia, New York, 1990) I included works by Kjell Espmark, Lennart Sjögren, Eva Ström and Tomas Tranströmer. In 1995 a fair-sized selection of Aspenström appeared in the *Quarterly Review of Literature* (Princeton, New Jersey). Aspenström, Espmark, Sjögren and Ström are represented here by recent work not included in any of the earlier selections. Since I have not previously included work by Söderblom in a book, the range of his poetry here is wider, from 1979 onwards.

To Swedish readers the omission of Tranströmer from even a small anthology of this kind would be surprising. My 'collected' Tranströmer was published by Bloodaxe (Newcastle) in 1986 and the newly published, updated edition of this includes my translations of his recent poetry. Tranströmer is indirectly present here, though, because many years ago he spoke highly of Lennart Sjögren's work, and encouraged me to try to translate some of it.

My justification for presenting these particular five poets, and not some other group of five or more, is purely subjective: I have followed their work with deepening interest over the years. I think the contrasts between them are enough to give variety to the grouping, and while I am all too aware of what is lost as their poems are lifted out of their native habitat I hope that at least some of their individual qualities can be gathered from my versions.

It is sad to have to record that Werner Aspenström died in January 1997. It seems that 'Dear Squirrel' was his last poem; he was working on it in the final week of his life.

R.F.

Kjell Espmark

Contents

Translator's Preface

Kjell Espmark (b.1930) was Professor of Comparative Literature at the University of Stockholm from 1978 to 1995; he became a member of the Swedish Academy in 1981 and chairman of its Nobel Committee in 1988. His seven books of criticism include studies of his fellow-poets Artur Lundkvist, Harry Martinson and Tomas Tranströmer, and an examination of the changing criteria in the choice of winners of the Nobel Prize in Literature. (The latter was published in an English version by G.K. Hall, Boston, 1991.) He has written a series of seven short novels, and eleven collections of poems.

After his first three collections his main poetic work went into two 'trilogies', the first appearing between 1968 and 1975, and the second between 1979 and 1984. The poems in these six books, or two sets of three, are richly interrelated — the reader constantly discovers echoes, parallels, variations not only within the detail of separate poems but also across the wide perspectives opened by the overall plan of the books. These connections are intended to be experienced as organic rather than schematic or mechanical. And however wide-ranging the field of reference may be, the immediate focus at any given point is nearly always an individual, and the individual is nearly always appealing directly to the reader. The poet himself is out of sight. If we want to, we could see this authorial withdrawal being predicted in a poem from his 1961 collection:

He himself steps hesitantly out of his work;
when the text is ready it disowns him.

The personae who confront us, or who ask us to confront
them, belong to widely scattered nationalities and historical
ages.

A reader coming to Espmark's poetry for the first time and
reading the above remarks before reading any of the poetry
may think either that such a learned man must write learned
and therefore difficult poems or that a man so busy with other
things can't have enough time left to write decent poems.
Neither supposition is true, yet notions of that sort do have a
way of surviving, like weeds that insist on returning. Tommy
Olofsson opened his introduction to Espmark's *Collected
Poems 1956-1984* (1987) by suggesting that there are two
Espmarks — one Kjell and one Professor Espmark. The latter
is indeed learned, and in control, while the former is not
entirely in control but has a restless heart that 'creates
life-giving confusion among the learned allusions' and threatens
to upset the balance of 'professorially elegant composition.'
This 'sabotage' enables the poet to achieve 'a striking and
immediate illusion of urgent reality.' The idea of dividing
Espmark into two is not a very credible one, but we can see
that Olofsson felt he had to dispel the type of preconception I
mentioned above.

In Espmark's second collection, published as long ago as
1958, there is a short piece about a literary scholar who is
staring through a magnifying glass at the worn seams in a dead
poet's suit:

> Look — on the knee, a stain! He scrapes at it
> with trembling hand. It all fits!
> He turns again to the immortal lines to Angela.
> Now he sees between the lines
> new words emerging.
> He clings to his desk
> blind with the clarity of his vision.
> Startled sparrows on the window-sill.

Espmark included this poem in his *Collected Poems* so he must have felt it to be part of his story and so it is, if we look past the obvious limits of the satire. With hindsight we can imagine these lines setting out what became one of Espmark's main themes: the rescue of the individual from oblivion. There are other themes, of course, waiting for the reader to discover, but if we must pick out one as a starting-point, this one will serve well. Over and over, in poems which could be described as first person posthumous portraits, the personae who grasp at the reader's attention are either in danger of losing their identity, or have already lost part of it, or indeed have almost lost it entirely. The only hope for the dead is the attention of the living: it is only in so far as we look at them that they can be seen, only in so far as we listen to them that they can speak to us. If we are blind and deaf to them, they vanish into oblivion, not to be recovered.

The cover picture of the *Collected Poems* offers an echo of the theme: it shows part of a fresco with dolphins rolling round, and the fresco, on Knossos, dates from around 1,600 B.C. The dolphins and their colours have survived so long, so it seems — yet there are stains, little smudges where oblivion is starting to nibble. The cover of *When the Road Turns* (1992) carries one of Cézanne's paintings, the one which the concluding poem of his collection lets us watch Cézanne struggle to create. For Cézanne doesn't simply copy the landscape he sees before him: laboriously, daub by daub, he has to force his *landscape* into being. He has to drag it out of oblivion; it can, naturally, fade back into oblivion. The fact that Cézanne made several versions of the same theme adds a little bonus to the appropriateness of the cover. What we see in the picture is not a unique final version, *the* created landscape, but only one of a number of possible variations, as if Cézanne were compelled to make repeated attempts, as if there were a whole series of (temporary?) *landscapes* to be extracted from the landscape.

Prague Quartet

1

So many listening. Seeming to recognize.
Like the castle on its hill — a scoured head
filled with suspicions, shelf upon shelf.
It's 1985 and will remain so.
The houses up there are hanging on
although they've long since lost their foundations.
Only the cathedral has weight and time,
half of it gusts of wind, half of it stone:
an old man with a stroke
fumbling for words to express his rage.

A devastation is at work here
which the senses can barely grasp
yet they find it surprisingly familiar.
As if thrashing wing-beats
and tearing claws ... No, the austere space
contradicts our presentiments:
'No more's happening here than Liberation!'

One piece of the past, at least, left:
John of Nepomuk being tumbled into the river
by hands which have failed to loosen his tongue.
As if frozen in a fall from a police office window.
Buttercups and carnations are heaped before his place
with an old-fashioned appeal:
'Free us from denunciation!'

Wing-beats and claws … It sounds
like a culture vanishing.
The scent of lilac is suddenly a phrase
and one more instalment inaccessible.

This street was once a piece of Europe.
So many languages, so many ways of thinking
and room for them in an ale-house
the size of an open hand.
The singing from the open window
wants listeners to recognize —
What do we mean by 'recognize'?

Those small remnants of flesh
constantly whirling out of nothing —
the air glossy as if full of black beaks.
The people crossing the bridge — how they thin out!

We move in towards the old square.
The walls scraped, dull parchment
fighting against its new text.
Instead of faces, scratches and hacks.
The crowd on the square stiffens: a gnashing of thoughts.
As if something tried to be understood.

2

The lovers are liberated slowly
from the suffocating evening.
The hotel room dissolving away.
Like the Ascension on the ceiling of St Nicholas':
they rise through the red smoke
in a stiffening whirl of sheets.
Legs hesitate a moment
dangling helplessly from the ecstasy
with magnified soles
before the azure absorbs them too.
Only the tottering houses are left,
arched into the sudden vacancy.

It's quiet. Gradually
shy faces in the plaster
emanate round the waking onlookers:
with sprawling fingers St Nicholas blesses
the money-changers in nervous jeans,
the double-bass master who lost his position
when he married in church,
the waitress struggling with the country's future —
a trayful of unwashable china.
Flaking faces, unexpectedly as close
as their own laboured breathing.

3

Here Kafka is a poltergeist.
Exorcized from the book-shops
he now haunts each street in Prague
(which then becomes a street in Prague).
It's told how the minister M one night
met himself on Charles Bridge.
He's still being treated for what he learnt.
And a bus-load of Party-members from Bratislava
on a hungry visit to government headquarters
vanished with an unknown guide. At times
they can be heard inside the walls.
Is that him with a vague smile
hanging a warning-sign by Laterna Magika?
(The street beneath the entrance is gone.)
I spell my way through the foreign text
and see how the theatre audience insists,
floating in over the shaft's nerves and veins,
Prague's opened rib-cage:
they leaf through a coming year,
discuss its protagonists.
As if a new production were inescapable
in the inescapably closed theatre.

4

The public spring condenses
in today's concert in St Nicholas'.
Such lavish orthodoxy! Trumpets.
The choir steadily dissolving
heralds the People's liberation
from the people. And holds back 1985.
Trombones. Up on the plinth
power in a golden mitre incidentally
named St Cyril of Alexandria.
Presses down his crozier on the throat
of the heretic, here called Nestorian.
The poor victim is bent backwards, bald with pain,
with holes instead of pupils.
Only the half-open mouth is alive —
his cry checked an inch before the stone.
But why those enormous ears?
Do we attribute to a choked dissident
such powers of hearing?

Fortissimo: the roof opens slowly
to the tornado of faith: the red haze
takes up its own into its kingdom.

Only a frightened scrap of sun
has reservations up in the gallery,
hovers by the organ which Mozart played.
That glimpse is enough! Clarifies
what the heretic's ears are waiting for:
a Beethovenian *Waldhorn*

in some corridor of the future. Hesitatingly
like a waking drunk clearing his throat.

Dreams! Czesław Miłos has just announced
that the order of Europe is as stable
as it was after the Vienna Congress.
But power is contemplating with its mitre off
preparing itself, just to be sure,
in case it is time for a quick change of clothes.

Ahead, perhaps a century away,
a freedom can be sensed so unbound
that anyone walking over Charles Bridge risks
being scattered with his own breath.
Then the demons will be driven from every house.
So long as excessive zeal doesn't force
the bookshop out of the word 'bookshop'
and the bridges out of the gloss 'bridge'.
The crozier will undoubtedly be broken that day
and the bald heretic will be free to speak.
But will the words succeed in leaving his mouth
any more than now, if there is no-one
concerned enough to listen
and scratched enough to recognize?

Questions. Questions.
It'll certainly be a hundred years
before we see liberation from Liberation.

Route Tournante

Cézanne has set up a sullen easel
in what does not yet exist.
He is so well-versed in the geology
of absence, layer by layer, that already
the nakedness of canvas is wholly authentic.

The road that turns in last year's grass
is still only a curve in the mind,
pilfered from an old Chinaman.
It originates in a grimy chapter
he has scraped away with his knife —
you were never there!

Begin with the shadows
and work in towards the brightening centre.
The blue-grey can entice a field back.

Like his life this treacherous year:
the throbbing foot that won't heal
and could consider leaving him.
While the road that wills, once more —
what thirst for the sun.

Among the women in dark head-scarves
his mother walks stooped in the dead man's grief.
When the others have vanished round a bend
she makes excuses
to hang on like a blue haze above the road.

So hard to bear another touch —

It's colour that can touch the world.
Of course he has mentioned logic. And the cone.
But these are approximate values.
No theory can get hold of
the furious energy inside things.
Only a grasp of colours
can force 'reality' to a response.

Dab by dab, a dogged colour-scale
lifting a village out of the village:
gables, a steeple, a possible road
and a fugue of swallows.
Each house is uninhabited: is waiting
for whoever can summon strength to return.

A day is a year.

Like his life —
took decades to see that verdure is blue.
And now in a moment or two he has managed
to paint the ringing of bells.

The brush sinks.
The canvas has forced a landscape to emerge
in what merely calls itself landscape.
And the road really turns.

Each second has a moist glint
no-one could see before.
He stands with his beating pain
in last year's grass that is suddenly fresh.

When a language dies ...

When a language dies
the dead die a second time.
The sharp word that turned the earth
in damply glistening furrows,
the chipped word with steaming coffee,
the bright and slightly flaked word
that for a moment reflected
the window and the noisy elm outside,
the secret sweet-smelling word
the hand sought in the dark
with shy assurances:
these words which gave the dead a life
beyond life
and the living a share in a greater memory
have just been scraped out of history.

So many shadows scattered!
Without a name to live in
they are forced into final exile.

The sign on the overgrown station
is called something with 54 letters

which no-one can get their mouth round any more.
That we could put up with.
If only all those
who died for the second time
had not taken the roughness of earth away with them,
the green from foliage, the coolness from the stream.
The foot can suddenly go right through the ground.
And no-one knows what the wind wants with us
or why we once came here.
Of course we can hear the birds in the tree
but what has become of the song?

How wrong, yet how persistent ...

How wrong, yet how persistent —
that Eurydice with a fading cry
would return to depths and darkness!
She recoiled — yes — from his terrified stare
for who'd want to be seen eight days after death?
Unwillingly, though, she did follow
that familiar stranger
who sang her out of facelessness
day after day after day
and overwhelmed her protests.
She lived long by his side
without living by his side.
Hard to understand
how she could drink a goblet of wine
without drinking a drop

or how she could walk in the sun
with steps groping in the dark.
Only the man she thought she loved
and reached for with hesitant finger-tips
seemed now and then to understand
when he embraced longing and air.

From **Jotted on History's Margin**

6

As if I were trying in vain to break free
of the faceless muttering darkness
pouring down the stairway,
landing by landing, century by century,
a darkness we know all too well.

In the hall inside the copper doors
all the thoughts ever thought have been piled up.
What a condensed odour of dust in the gloom!

In the centre, the sarcophagi.
Like those of the Ming Dynasty
but smaller and more faded.
My skin starts twitching by the third one:
I sense I must be by my own waiting grave.
But the guide, who has read my associations,
shakes his head and explains
in a voice hoarse with history
that this is the grave I've just stepped out of.

7

This is one of history's ambushes.
For several hours or days
Leningrad has taken back its name.
And the policeman is leafing in my pocket-diary,
going through my memory line by line.
'May I explain, off the record ...'
'There is no *off the record* here!'
The hand sweeps towards the Neva, the famished warehouses
the floating palaces, the uniforms
shivering in queues at the ferry.
He is sitting inside the answer.
But turns pages: suspects I have copied down
that line in Marx that cancels Marx.
I look at his hands,
the lead ring, and recognize
the Mesopotamian temple-ministrant
whose face kept the kingdom intact.

From *Illuminations*

2

The children are sitting beside each other
curiously white
in a white room at a white piano.
It is yet is not our dining-room.
Their hair is so white the eye recoils.
They laugh when bottom line and top line
unexpectedly concur.
The music too seems white.
The children must be fifteen and twelve.
Hard to decide
since they weigh nothing
and the picture denies us a context.
But there's something wrong with the light.
It is much too intense
also for these high windows.
Then we can see how the white wallpaper
darkens at the edges, curls
and lets through a flame, then one more, and one more.

Four Greek Voices from under the Ground

1

I am the most lonely of shadows.
The others avoid me
like the stench of an unhealing sore.
They won't even let me carry a name
for fear of contagion. You think you know
I am the one who showed history the way
and let the Persians attack us from behind
at the pass in whatever it is now called.
The others down here won't even soil their thoughts
through acquaintance with my deceit. No-one
will admit I served Necessity,
that god who forces events
towards an end hidden from us
and demands we turn a deaf ear
when the skulls crumble like shells.
I wanted in a word to serve something greater
than human loneliness.

2

Death was said to be glorious when bravely you fall to the fore.
There was nothing glorious
to the man already on his knees
in the slash from behind on the shoulder-blade
or in the stab in the genitals.

Nothing glorious either about the women
who came by night
and snatched from me the fumbled picture
of the woman I never stopped loving
but search for in vain down here
without the picture to serve as my memory.
Have I been straying for one year or a thousand?
One thing I do know: I'm tireless in my search
for whoever wrote about that glorious death.
I've saved this little knife,
a rarity down here,
to slit the tongue out of his mouth.

3

Do you know it's your misunderstanding
that plagues us dead most of all?
I'm a simple statue, the flat sort,
a woman with crossed arms
and a face scarcely begun,
but I'm not on that account without feelings.
To me it's torture when you late barbarians
who have exhibited my nakedness
maintain I served fertility
or showed the way to the final kingdom.
No, I was put in the loved one's grave
by the woman who didn't dare follow him
yet wouldn't abandon him to loneliness.

I was the one to get kisses of mud
and caresses of naked bone
intended for a living being.
Only a heart of stone could bear that.

4

Not even the *name* Porphyry should have survived.
That I am still now and then glimpsed among you
is due to the diligence of my enemies.
Just come a little closer.
It's not that my voice is timid
but it has been forced to take such diversions
that the words are as worn as old sandals.
My writings of my own cause have been burnt
by those who had a better point of view
and my thoughts taken away to be broken on the wheel
by my pious opponents.
What rescued me for the future
is their need to contradict me —
I reach you through their criticism.
If they had drowned me in the silence of the well,
tossed my books to the pigs
and given no hint of my opinions
then no cunning could have helped me this far.
It's their zeal to silence me
which lets you hear my voice.

But don't expect
to see my face.
Whoever has to find his way
out of overwhelming argument
and grinding mockery
can't lay claim to much substance.
You will have to make do
with half a smile here,
an over-experienced wrinkle there.
Between 'neither' and 'nor'
you will still sense my breathing.

The Other Life

As if standing beside a burned out car
and seeing one's body crumpled over the wheel —
Today's like a normal October Saturday
but belongs to another calendar.
I seem to have groped out of my life
and stumbled into my *life*.

The same insubstantial maples and ash-trees.
The same haze with the same promises.
And the grass claims to bear our footprints.
But we've never been here before.
Digging holes for tulip bulbs you see
the earth being created beneath the spade.
While I shut off the water for winter
and hear water drip for the first time ever.

Jackdaws from an erased year
insist, insist
and persuade the field to a new attempt
still only a newly ploughed gleam.

Words like 'chronology' and 'explanation'
are rusty tools I put by in the shed.
Reason can appeal to a higher court.

The other life
with the roads we never walked
must have existed all the time

an arm's length distant
with the *sea* resounding beside the sea —
but not for him who reached out to it.
The word is grace.

The wind turns
beyond what is still smouldering
and the eyes learn that smoke can sting:
the life I didn't choose
has suddenly chosen me.
And I am unwritten.
Write me.

The Day We Buried Foucault

That inexorable black sun
has a fitting place in the calendar.
The shop grilles are of course locked —
what's one not tempted to sell today?
One is nervous too in a city
so full of streets where no-one dared to walk.
And do we know a whit about the sewage system?
The Palais de Justice is a daring hypothesis.

At the café table a German philosopher
with a moustache like a drying-up waterfall
mutters his 'noch einmal' over his glass.

But whoever is looking for his other life
will have to entice an unused year
which has not been split into madness and insight.
The seventeenth century seeps out of the walls
with a convincing taste of metal.
In logic there still lives an unreasonable love.
And Paris is more than a text.

Waving gloves of misted plastic
the policeman in the middle of Boul' Mich
tries to redirect the flow of history.
The bridge too is enveloped in plastic
against the saliva stench of the Seine.
Perhaps also from fear of the muttering
of this collective memory.

Admitted: our knowledge of humanity
must again be founded on hell.
The dogs stand still and listen to a cry
that passes far above the human ear —
the glass I raise to the sniffling German
shatters and cuts my hand.
He shies from the blood.

Then we'd see reason
groping on all fours
for its trampled spectacles
while madness finds refuge in its scream.
Neither has found the other.

Of course. Everything can be traced back
to the grid of knowing, to be glimpsed
even in the cracked concrete —
everything but what really happens.
Islam swept down in the gutter
floats slowly upwards.

In this infernal light one can see
how thought has been placed under wardship.
But resistance also is brought out in relief.
Each stone is a prisoner on hunger strike.

Life for Sale

The wooden fence gives up its cracked resistance
and buyers stroll in the tall grass, peeping
on tiptoe through the fly dirt on the windows.
There he sits, rooted to the kitchen table
among potato peelings and bored empties.
The shadows of his parents
try to smuggle away the food scraps
and make him sit up straight:
'He was just going to see to the nets.'
But the son is unsteady as the squint privy door
that comes loose in a speculator's hand.
He knows. Out there the trees are staggering with fruit.
But he has no longer hands to pluck it.

The dead appeal now like brokers:
'Listen, so much life in the walls,
life we hadn't the heart to live.
And feel here with your hand —
so much knowledge round the empty calf-pen,
so much decency in the pruned trees.
Life that wants to move on, compulsorily,
and lost patience with that fellow in the kitchen
and his woman, who should have been flaunting her belly.

Of course he hears, the lignified farmer,
how stairway and out-house haggle.
But can't be bothered butting in.
Breathing, after all, costs 13%.

And the treachery is completed.
The pump and the barn have turned their backs on him
and smirk ingratiatingly
at whoever is most likely to bid highest.
The gossip of the centuries in the walls
agrees to every conceivable latex-paint
and centuries of footsteps are ready for the sander.
The dead come to meet the newcomers
and try to breathe with their lungs.

That fellow at what was recently a table
is so abandoned by the things of the farmyard
he can no longer catch sight of the fireplace.

Even the food scraps and last year's newspaper
move off away from him
towards a new attempt.

Letter Writing

1

Half the letter is written
by the person it is sent to.
You, waiting for my lines —
there's so much you already know about me
that I am too close to see.
So much you can tell me
through my scribbling hand.
From the paper before me there rises
a murmuring like the noise
from headphones laid aside.

2

I wrote to Nichita Stănescu
not knowing he'd just died.
Felt an alien chill rising
from the writing up through my hand.
Such a lack of sense-impressions in the room!
I forced his image to appear in the wallpaper:
his puffed features which had learnt too much,
the smile where the poem had vanished,
the feet that had given notice to the shoes.

But the frost rose up my arm.
The frozen words on the page
repelled their meaning.
Halfway through, the letter was over.

3

So much wiser the writing
than the writer.
These lines become more and more oblique
and the message altered into something
neither of us intended.
The last part will maybe break loose
and describe something beyond both of us —
our turned-away history, so valid
that our faces dare to leave us.

Family Memory

When the blind war was over
a farmer from Red Island was condemned
to block and wheel
for the crime of hailing the king that lost.

His wife walked from Jämtland to beg
mercy from the proper Majesty.
With shrinking heart and bleeding feet
she reached Stockholm in time.
Stopped the king at the city gate,

her hand on the stirrup: 'Gracious Lord — '
And His Magnificence, the sun into his breast
as the horse reared, was pleased
to grant her her husband's head
in confirmation thereof setting
a stern seal on the bill of pardon.

With steps that dared to love again
she turned back north.
But arriving at last
after stony weeks she found
no boat on her side of the strait.
Everyone had crossed the water
to see how it fares with a man
from whom God has turned His face.
And so she stood with rigid lips
on the mainland shore and saw
in the distance her husband's head fall.

Archetype

The picture in the cave
has been lifted into the paper:
Chinese monk rides a fish
as big as a boat.
Outstretched leaves on his bamboo staff
depict the speed. His eyes and mouth
are opened wide by the water's resistance.
But the figure itself is stillness

and the bridle in his hand invisible:
he rides as if he weren't riding.
Both are red, the monk an assemblage
of leathery doctrines
he smilingly disclaims,
the fish a fusion of scales and surprise
— the round eye knows it belongs
to a lower realm of horror and madness.
So together they manage to transform
the white world around them:
bubbles, creases, beginnings,
already emerging from the frame.

Caribbean Quartet

1.

This copper engraving from 1900
has burns and curled edges
as if about to break into flame.
But the frigate bird soars out of the paper
and in again, draws away, comes back
irrespective of what the picture is aware of.
No, the eruption has not yet happened.
At the same time the volcano is erupting.
And Saint-Pierre with its human mass,
with ships, chickens and fluttering clothes-lines
is in the midst of its luxuriating life
buried in horror and pumice.
A lady in black with an umbrella
held up against the rain of fire
is just alighting from a mule-drawn tram —
she has all the time in the world
although the rails are already bent by the heat.
'It's only me who knows,' cries the paperboy,
this cavity in the lava.

Thought is captive in the engraved pattern.
The leap belongs to philosophy.
And the only one free
is the prisoner behind a metre-thick wall
sleeping himself sober while time melts.

Clad in amazed mercy
he'll be exhibited in the cities of Europe
as the man who survived history.
People will finger and measure and photograph
this inconceivable other life.

The real prisoners throng outside the prison-bars
among the merciless lines of the engraving,
laughing, calling, inside the stone.

Outside the peep-hole a hand's breadth of sky
and a fraction of a second:
the frigate bird.

2.

Caribbean rain:
like falling mightily in love
with what we've loved for long —
suddenly I'm standing in the dark.
The rain smoothes out my features
and washes out my eye-holes,
beats right through my rib-cage
and drums on my pelvis
that steams in helpless confusion.
There are no words.
The rain on fossil lips
makes language obsolete.
An invasion to be read as liberation.

In full sunlight this darkness
which can't exist but does.
And that is the first day of creation.

3.

You who are close as sweat on the forehead
but live in another fold of time:
hold us — so we're not snatched by the wind
and scattered among the centuries.
You who tend the fields by night
with inward-gazing eyes
and faint smiles that know the way,
you who mend the broken fences
and prevent misfortune while we sleep,
you who polish the words while waiting for dawn:
don't lose patience with us.
Without you bread would not be bread,
without you the ground would be friable as sugar,
without you language would turn its back on us.
Your death turns our life into life.
Hold us tight with your chilled hands.

4.

I open the shutters with stiff fingers:
for someone who has slept in a monument
it is hard to break free of the stone.
A changeling city. Old Havanna
turns its worn face to the sea
and daren't show its teeth in a smile.

'The Revolution Continues!' shout the posters.
In the cracked glue beneath them
we can read the lower revolution
the one that makes the dictator drop his glance
in case the eyes of others will steal his strength.
'The world may sink,' his fist says,
'if only I can define the ending.'
The loudspeakers multiply in the trees.

The blockade is now in its hundredth year.
The people are living on beans and air
and the bitter drink of experience.
No thought can be thought to a conclusion.
The street-lamp also makes its contribution to the darkness.

Once the capital was moved here.
Now they have moved the concept of man
to the shrinking area within the walls.
The forbidden city outside
is populated by sceptical shadows
who've seen too much and are called the dead.

Boys who are only sketches for boys
and in the meantime live between the stones
prowl hungrily round the visitors
to snatch their language and experiences.
And the threadbare war ministry
retrains as a museum
without the guards noticing.

I've stopped short before a bad painting
of a memorial service in 1828
with the gentlefolk in blue and white Empire style
and the populace like clinging apes behind the fence —
masters like slaves trapped in the pattern.
I myself am trapped in another pattern,
held together by stiffening thoughts.
But in mid-afternoon a crack opens
for another freedom than Freedom:
a woman in the picture looks this way sidelong
and her glance sinks in mine,
Only seconds separate us.

The frigate bird soars out of her time
into mine
and back into hers.

Lennart Sjögren

Contents

Translator's Preface

Lennart Sjögren (b.1930) lives on Öland, where he was born and grew up. Öland is a long narrow island in the Baltic, close to the south east coast of Sweden. Many of Sjögren's paintings are full of light, from the sky and from the sea. The language of his poems, even when they deal (as they usually do) with the most tangible subjects, has a certain airiness of texture, letting the light through. The idea of open space round lines is one he has mentioned to me in letters; and, indeed, a Swedish reviewer of his latest collection remarked on how his words come 'with the right amount of air between'.

That is particularly relevant to his longer sequences, part of his work which he seems to feel is important to him for such pieces make up most of a *Selected Poems* he compiled in 1980. He has compared the long poem to a panorama painting (which is inclusive and apparently static) and the short poem to a still-life (limited in motif and range); he added that in the short poem, as in the still-life, 'the view inwards' is 'clarified in a quite unsuspected manner'. Both the clarity and the unsuspected manner in which we discover it are characteristics of the best of his short poems. Even when they are patently complete, we still feel something has been opened. Whether short or long, his poems belong together; they are parts of a continuum where nature is recognisable but not predictable.

The Oar

The finder of a smashed oar
can't with certainty say
that a foundering has taken place

but it's likely there's a rower
out on the water

a forgetfulness can have happened to him
his name
he surrendered to the current
and renounced the possibilities of the oar.

A simple example, maybe, from his 1984 collection, but useful enough to start with: the concrete situation, and the unanswered questions. And the site: the shore as a meeting place for different worlds and what often makes the meeting dramatic is the sheer physicality of the worlds that meet.

Yet solidity of any kind, and especially of the man-made sort, is deceptive: human artefacts have a built-in obsolescence determined not by their maker but by nature. In Sjögren's 1987 collection of short prose pieces (*Kopparkrukan*, The Copper Pot) we can follow a chronological account of how the waves demolish a stranded boat; we can watch a copper pot folding with age as if on a speeded-up film; we can watch and hear a wooden house rotting internally according to its own laws. In the opening piece in the book, rigid asphalt is far from rigid, as observed by (gleeful?) bats:

Many believe that the ground beneath the asphalt has settled once and for all and that no further movements from below can break the rigid surface. Perhaps that is why the bats hang upsides-down. They point downwards and hear how small white fungi, softer than spittle, are growing upward and will soon cause cracks in the roadway.

When that happens and the asphalt starts to boil, the bats will rise with a shriek, they'll laugh like fledglings and swing off to shout across the earth: 'Now it's begun!'

The animals in Sjögren's poems may be fascinating or horrifying to us, peaceful or manic, but they are stubbornly alien, totally absorbed in a world which ignores us. When we intrude it is usually with a knife: even then, when the carcase is opened up 'like a triptych', totally exposed, the flesh doesn't seem to have the last word.

Sjögren's latest collection (*Deras ögon* 1994, Their Eyes) 1994) contains three related sequences from which it is difficult to give satisfactory extracts — individual pieces may seem fragmentary but they are open to each other and work cumulatively. The three parts are devoted respectively to a calf, a fish and a cat: the calf, taken out to be slaughtered, is recalled from childhood, the fish is the source of both fish-meal and symbolic meaning, and the cat, a miserable outcast on the streets of Rome, seems to be surviving. At one point the cat, the four-legged creature, says to the two-legged one: 'Come with me to the queen of the sewers.' One of the places to which the fish leads us is, of course, the catacombs. And after the transfiguration of the calf into meat, there is a vision of the muzzle reappearing, coming up out of the earth, and it is hard to tell if this is a resurrection or a haunting.

Pike Head

What sharp teeth you have: Pike head
although the sun has roasted you against the wall
although winter has skinned you
although you've now been hanging there for three years.

Others have their Progress
others have their Sergeant.
I have you.

Your head is devoid of everything
that might suggest friendliness.
Yet I'd count you
as one of my closest friends
one with whom I can talk
in the language of the speechless.

You certainly don't belong to the demonic
and not to the apocalyptic either.
You are what you are
what you are is you.

Nor would I count myself
among the adorers of animals
just because I keep company with you.
I don't worship you, yet you belong
to the ranks of the comforters.

Your route was straight from the watery depths
to that air which is man's but not yours.
Nor did you ask for mercy
either in my eyes or in the eyes of others.

And what you said in silence as you were hauled up
I don't know.
You've no eyes left, and hardly any skin
but your teeth
slowly eating their way through the sun's heat
you are still baring them at me.

Topography

The fox tracks are as usual streaked with blood
like the human tracks.

The forest round about is sleeping
likewise the streets.
The night is now truly deep
whoever screams will scream in vain.

Frost ices over the trees
and the blind eyes of the neon signs.

A spring-trap has been set in the forest
a knife is waiting on the window-sill
for whoever needs it.

Between Evening and Night

This evening the words as well as
the remaining trees lack their weight
tonight the houses free themselves
from their foundations.
No-one's surprised at that.
Yet everyone is surprised
and thinks
that an axis different from the usual one
is now being threaded through the earth
cancelling its weight.

The Cry

A small stone statue
and a tiny bird
rest in a black space quite different
from the one we see here above the roofs.
It could be anything from a desert night
down to a velvet embroidery.
A white and seemingly unopened pyramid
stands on the horizon.

Bird — do you also feel loss
in such loneliness
or are you already nailed down like a dead insect
on the black sky.

Then a door into the pyramid opens.

You fly in among the mummified people
and hear your own voice calling to you
further and further in.
Or is it your stone friend
who now wants to tell you something
after all the silence out there
in the other blackness.

The Wound

In what other landscape than this
could evening produce such weight.
The horses that come to drink
have large wounds

yet no war
has passed this way.

What desire to sink
rises from the water
and the humans have been quite abandoned
by the trees.

The Calf

One morning a big-eyed calf
is down on the shore
to drink.
The old sea-charts show a different shore.
Something the calf doesn't know.

With its eyes wide open it drinks
and as always by still water
the calf is met by another calf
from the watery depths.
And their eyes and their muzzles
drink from the same hand.

An Unusually Clear and Mild Day

I saw the snow unusually clear and mild that day
with a tinge of a more deceptive
and older light.
The red spot
which I thought was from a rowanberry
was bird's blood.
The long night arrived unusually early that day.

The Light

Birds wounded by shot
are more often to be seen
on our coasts
along with the more strong-winged.

Sometimes the rainbow spreads out its light
behind them.

About Her Love

Like so many others
this century and earlier
I also asked:
what is there outside the bounds of the universe
where the rainbow breaks?

Those who knew replied:
there you'll find Nothing.
And I asked:
what's hiding outside Nothing?

The one we call Night
replied:
there
a woman can walk
with an armful of fresh grass.

About her age
about her love
about what kind of grass
I ask no more.

Snail-time

Now when the snails are again appearing in the grass
and on their silent backs carrying away
part of my life too
while the uneaten apples return to the ground.

Autumn is waiting
winter is waiting beyond it
and the ceaseless mouths in the lower soil
are already preparing for
a new summer.

I thought then that the world stood still
that I'd misunderstood time's conditions
and that my anxiety
confusedly fingered its coat as if it belonged
to some unknown passer-by.

Hazy

Night climbs down from the trees
morning still hesitates in a haze
yellow straw is burning on the fields.

Something has been told to me of life
but far from all
something I have known by its scent
but far from all.

Across the winter snow a chimera like a hare hops off
half four-legged
half human. Its eyes shine.

The Teeth

All the fish teeth, all the dog teeth
and all the man teeth.

All those who were born, all the living
all the dead
and the teeth that accompany them.

All the grass with its teeth
all the stones
in the course of ages
gnawing themselves down.

They all eat their way forward
chewing the lives of others.
The sun's tooth in the centre and the moon's beside it.

In eating is their art
in eating they have what they have
nothing else is theirs.

At last they're in the horse's jawbone
slanting splinters
brittle, reaching out to life's departure.

About the World

About the world which was never created
because it was always there
about a night calling to another night
and about a lake whose waters are running out.

About the spider webs that wait each morning
and the fly's step that resembles our own
when the spider approaches.

About the sewage that seeps up
from the underground
and the trees its beautiful sisters.

About the time-pieces ticking in our heads
and about the animals pricking up their ears

in the winter nights
about our clockwork which coincides
with that of the minerals.

Still

I still believe that bird exists.
It has followed me now year after year
sometimes like a tiny starved skeleton
or even like a puffy flake of soot.
Sometimes like a beak rapidly glimpsed
from beneath
from which no sound can be expected.

It is more lonely than a wind-driven gull
and slighter than a sparrow
its call is more of a whimper
and its freedom is far away.

It hops aside alertly
in the heat of the traffic
and when it is run over it lets its body
be pressed into the asphalt
and its cry can be heard again
far away in another wood.

Dreamt for a Long Time

Dreamt for a long time
that I was travelling among the bedouins
we journeyed from morning to morning
from night to night

the mirages surrounded us

if we worshipped any god
it was the grain of sand
that which sets the deserts in motion.

Waves

Here come the waves on their way towards land
they are so many
and before I manage to say their names
and their first place of residence
they've gone.

What do they want of me?

That could no doubt be answered by those
who possess instinct.
I do not possess instinct.

Furthest away at the world's outer limit
they are watched over by wild animals.

The Moth

One day as I sat going through
old papers
or perhaps old clothes
a moth came up on my hand
it looked at me
folded its wings
and said
winter has now overtaken the world.

The Wood-Eater

You'll have seen the Wood-Eater
the one that eats through the walls by night
and then into our bodies
and then into our hearts.

You'll have seen how its eyes
have no pupils
how they close over a black well.

We lie troubled on our beds
listening
to the walls being eaten from inside
sweat forces its way out.

We can hardly make out the curtains
in the starlight

the small dreams turn into heavy stones
impossible to clamber over
a fly turns into a queenlike vulture.
Then the Wood-Eater comes.

The Straw-Rick

A straw-rick from The Middle Ages
came and took root in my soul,
lesser rats found a home there
they came and went.
An aeroplane propeller
from a futuristic exhibition
was also among the household utensils.

There were many things mixed together.

So long as a weasel didn't come
or a storm scatter the straw
everything was as usual.

Coastline

This piece of coast was late
in floating up from the sea
and therefore lacks both older and younger stone-ages
according to the geologists
it will soon return to the water.

Its rock is porous
slanting birches line the shore.

The birds that call out of the evening
say it's already too late.

Sunsets are splendidly unrestrained
they make us think of The Book of Revelation
and of the swilled blood in modern slaughterhouses.

The Head

Found a calf's head in the water
held it up
asked as one usually asks:
Who did you live for, calf
who did you die for
who separated your head
from the rest of the world.

The head replied
as heads usually reply:
Who I was
and who I came from
who removed my body, and why
— that was your question.

Then the water changed
it turned into a bellowing cow
that bled.

Someone in the meantime had placed a knife
in my hand.

A Cat with Wings

A cat with wings
very like Silence
enters in the evening, asks:
may I stay here a while
is there a fish here
or some soul to eat
and may I bring my night
in with me?
In return you can hear
how I purr
as I curl my claws in sleep
and my wings retract
in my fur.

In the Gravel-Pits

In the gravel-pits
and in the bottomless swamp-lands
they all live:
the remnants of bone
the remnants of tree
the remnants of hair
and the dried-in family wars.

Any other sort of land
I for one did not
catch sight of.

The Crossroads

Compare the night to a black cart
and the morning to a capsized carriage
but what images would do
for the uncertainty we feel
at a crossroads
like this one
where a blind child leads
a wooden horse.

The Tree

The tree approaches like a huge bird and lands on the plain. It seems to have just taken hold in the ground when the train passes. The wings are still extended, bearing summer's every leaf.

There is silence all around, a silence which only the plain can induce. If there were any noises to be heard, they would vanish anyway in the clattering of the rails.

The tree does not possess the train's freedom to move on from landscape to landscape, but long after it is out of view the passengers remember how the leafy crown observed them and how the motionless wings were still there in their waiting.

from *The Calf*

First the wound in the forehead
then the wound in the throat.

Then you were opened wide.

As the altar doors are opened out
on feast days
so you were opened this morning for us
you showed us
what was inside you
We made sure of what to us
is edible
we consigned to earth what to us
is not edible.

You are the opened one
opened wide for us
yet quite inaccessible.

Then your head was also taken from you.

The starlings gathered the sun in their bodies
that day you were taken out
and the lime-tree tops were raised above the earth
in their new greenery.

The organ. The player, and the listener.

The crows — those who keep watch
sat further off in the tree.
The wheel drove past on the road.

I touched your muzzle
and witnessed the preparations for your death:
the knife
the hammer
the rope.

You had scarcely begun life
I had scarcely either.

Now you've been led out
seeing the sun for the first time.
You have taken up your position.
I watched, a witness
the trees were witnesses
the wind was a witness.

The butcher was like you the chosen one.

I have later wondered where The Plough
was that morning
— perhaps askew over China.
The evening star
which during the night becomes morning star
had surrendered to daylight
and was invisible.

You were listening
you stretched your head forward
as you did when you sucked
and thus stood convenient for the hammer.
You heard the summer whispering.

A great blind eye appeared
it reached over all of the earth
and whoever
weeps will continue to weep
and whoever received joy as his share
will continue in joyfulness.

Then the blind eye turned round
but did not see now either
— not as we do.

Bleeding, your muzzle rises again
out of the earth.

from *The Fish*

Fish
you swim through the catacombs
and with your fins penetrate stone
then plunge out of sight in the deep water
— the water scarcely to be heard
murmuring beneath the stone.
Behind you
you leave the sign
interpreted: the one returning through death.

You live in the sand beds
you live in the wild currents
where the vessels founder.

You are caught
ground to flour, displayed in the frozen food counters.
You carry a hook in your mouth
you carry it like a crozier.

You disappear.
In the disappearing you have your life.
You return.
In the returning you have your life.

In the middle is our place.
We often thought we came from
another census district
but from there we've been banished.

Sometimes when you open your slanting jaw
and break the otherwise unmoving
evening waters
we think some reconciliation is possible
— or at least a pact.

You whip up a storm then
and the waves roll away with lacerated backs
where the rainbow renders its complete repertoire
and as for the drowned
— no-one bothers to count them.

In the middle where we live there is no tranquility.
Fish
have you somewhere else you can show us?

When you open your jaws and swallow the world
and fill the cities with terror
— that is one variant.
When you filter the tiniest of creatures
through your teeth
and sleep right through all the wars
like a stone on the sea bed slime
— that is another variant.

Are you in a waking trance?

Your mouth is a packet of needles
as you wait motionless
if you tremble it's only the currents
caressing your body.

We thought you had disappeared
we thought you no longer existed.

You give us a lesson in non-tranquility.

You entangle yourself, you free yourself
you flicker backwards
against a cobalt-black darkness
and in nights that resemble gallows-hills.

If you could even blink in the sunlight
as the rest of us do:
the rats can, the deer, the polecats.
Likewise the martyrs
and their executioners.

It is part of our life
you are outside.

You made your eye into the globe
that watches over the world.

You belong to the watchman fraternity
where life weighs against life, death against death.

At Night

I'm not saying life is good
I'd rather say it was bad
yet I'm not saying that either.

I wish for only three implements:
set-square, scissors, knife-blade

so that I can measure and cut out
the things that can be measured

leaving the rest for the night to cut out
and the animals that then emerge.

In October

When car tyres screech
to a stop
and the noise may be likened
to a death-struggle between wild animals
in the depths of the forest

when the rain in October
becomes small slanting pin-pricks beyond good and evil
and the eel's skin darkens before its long journey

and when the wind repeatedly slams the doors
of an abandoned manor-house
or an equally abandoned kiosk
on a deserted beach

and the death-struggle whether now in earnest
or more theatrically intended
continues at the street corner and in the forest depths
while the rain falls —

with the back of your hand brush away an unease.

The Starfish

Sank deeper and deeper
where I heard the starfish at their mumbling.

Of the sea's love and madness they sang,
of things so bad
they are beyond human understanding,
of sodden driftwood
reaching bottom at last
— and much else we do best not to mention.

It was late and the sun's brightness
floated further and further away
on the surface of the water.

There was nothing that could shine right down to the seabed
and the seabed was very like our picture of Hades
with all those people crouching
along the street of death
where each name is offered oblivion.

But the starfish — their singing I'll remember.

Eva Ström

Eva Ström

Eva Ström

Translator's Preface

Eva Ström grew up on Lidingö, on the outskirts of Stockholm, and then settled in Kristianstad, in the south east of the country, in the area where her father's people had belonged. She worked as a doctor from 1974 to 1988 and then gave up medicine in order to write. She has produced poems, radio and stage plays, and short novels. Her writings are not voluminous but they are compact and intense and highly individual. They are all of a piece, too, the genres being close to each other: her novels and her poems often explore similar themes and do so by way of similar language. Throughout her work she moves in and out of roles or personae; in her earlier poems some of these roles are at first sight familiar (Snow White, The Sleeping Beauty, The Queen, The Prince) but her variations and juxtapositions are not exactly predictable.

Commenting in an interview on the impulse to write, she referred to 'a kind of irritation: you want to catch experiences that language is not up to. Then you almost have to abandon language, turn to dreams, myths, the subconscious, and it is there I find my material, before the brain has got hold of it and sorted it out, removing some things, interpreting others, making the material compatible with the current ideological or social veneer.'

Her poems have therefore often been described in terms of abrupt contrasts, of the tensions generated between opposites — the romantic and the enlightened, magic and reason, restraint and liberation, health and sickness... True enough, but what we have here is no schematic play. Something of the sensibility at work can be gathered from her account of her reaction to Rilke. As if in self-defence, she has experienced a strong resistance to the *Duino Elegies* for these poems have no effect if read in an unengaged manner, 'but to be drawn into their magnetic field is to have your world-image broken down. These are poems that pull you up by the roots ... They reawaken in me a peculiar memory of terror and intensity, when as a child I have a momentary visit from an angel and I scream until it disappears.'

We can gather a like impression from, for example, the following few lines, lifted out of context, from a poem called 'The Laughing Electrons' in her latest collection:

> The old compass needle swings round.
> Does the south pole exist? The north pole?
> Did someone come and rob us of magnetism?
> The real periodic system has been exchanged
> for a new chemistry with strange elements
> they taste salt and acrid, bloody and familiar.

Lines like these indicate a sense of fundamental disturbance in which our experience of both the familiar and the unfamiliar has a rawness that frightens and exhilarates. If Eva Ström's poems are allowed to work their way under the reader's skin, that is the kind of effect they have. And it seems that the poems themselves arise from experience of a like immediacy: they have been worked at, of course, being linguistic artefacts, but they give a strong sensation of flesh and nerve-ends.

Leave Me Alone

Leave me alone! This is nothing for me.
I hate that trembling song, all that wetness
I have to wade through, that fleshy darkness.
Make it simple.
I've no prayer about this,
just take away the bestiary,
the pelican that stabs its own heart
the Egyption rat that kills the crocodile

The death sentence is commuted to everlasting imprisonment
and the bread is ready
Also the water, the stone-age axe, the man who is frightened
by the photographs,
the woman suckling a wild pig

The elevation of the land is continuing, I feel it in my crown
the landscape is naked, rough and wet after the dragging ice
it looks at itself in surprise as if it had given birth
I can still miss that white pressing weight
spring is soggy and lacerated

Foucault's Pendulum

In foreign newspapers I read about professors
who long for the Middle Ages, for what was then
holy
as if it were a university or a library
within them a pendulum hangs
a great blasphemy by Foucault
showing that earth rotates
Only the pendulum is fixed
suspended in nothing.

The Bleeding Church-Organ

The depressed people pushed further into the department stores
huddled beneath the stalactites of the elevators
they held hands, they clutched their throats.
They tried in vain to shield themselves from the intruding light.

The pain had begun to leave the clothing
you could wrap a scarf round your neck without thinking
of whoever it had once belonged to, the identity scent had gone.
The dressed-up little girls wept in their white collars.

The holy Dorothy was called upon by a woman in labour.
In the middle of childbirth she took her place in the church roof,
freed herself of the vertical organ music, began dancing.
Small drips fell, branches beat against each other, drums rolled.

Jesus, chubby and round-thighed, listened in surprise from the
pulpit.
Those digital screams, did they still sound like human voices?
Was there still someone there at the big organ actually playing it?
Or had the organist abandoned the organ-loft leaving the
tape-recorder running?

The child was to be born, totalitarian, almighty and bloody.
Nothing worked with such autonomy as the big birth-giving
muscle.
The talking animals fell silent with all their speaking-with-tongues.
The new energy had nothing to do with their will.

The Radiant Ears of Corn

After hymns and sermon the book-pyre was lit.
The uprooted bramble broke out of the grave.

The pages burned. Soot flakes fluttered on the wind.
The murdered women all had first-names.

It was in the crèche the rape happened.
The mysterious person took shape and started singing.

She had a thread in her hand. She had met monsters.
The True Congregation was reading The Acts of the
Apostles.

The burnt books were valued at 50,000 silver drachmas.
The evil spirit had maltreated them naked and bloody.

The parachutes were released. The orthodox found
themselves on the pages of newspapers.
There was no longer any market for small silver temples of
Artemis.

The one road darkened and coiled its way out of history.
A new cross-breed grain took shape. In amazement the
people watched the radiant ears of corn.

The Enclosed City

The animals felt uneasy sooner than the humans did.
They wandered in huge herds out into the sunset.
The white raven flapped its wings.

The court was filled by the friends of both victim and
murderer.
They had all taken time off from school.
Small Japanese women determined the chicken's sex.

For the sake of egg production all the male chicks were
killed.
They hung in surprise for a moment on the conveyor belt
before being ground down in the rubbish-grinder.

The eighteen-year-old murderer drew a comic strip of the
murder.
Both he and the victim were turned into match-stick men.
The girl had no sex but a rectangular skirt.

Her throat is bare. The city besieged.
The goat with the gold teeth slaughtered.
The lorries are trying in vain to approach the enclosed city.

She had Left her Post

The nurse wept.
She had left her post and seen that the patients
could live without her, could die without her. In surprise she
looked at
the syringe, the medicines that continued into
the people's bodies.

The illnesses did not stop. They changed character but
continued into the houses, caring nothing for
lock or door, caused floods, stains on the floor,
shivers, insomnia and a dark apathy.

Quietly she watched what was happening. Saw the people grow
old,
flicker to life and become younger. Find new lovers,
consolation for
the scream of mucous membranes and the insolent waltz of the
seasons.
On streets aged twins walked around tending
their new-born puppies.

The Solo Yachtsman

The epileptic gave an animal shriek and fell in cramps.
The shop staff rang for an ambulance.
His legs were no longer twitching, slowly he came to his
senses.

Jesus came walking. He spoke about evil spirits. When the
man
rose from his stunned daze and the ambulancemen came
carrying the stretcher he was speaking about marvels and faith.

In the crypt the miracle was repeated.
The priest lectured on self-abandonment.
An inverted Our Father coiled out of their mouths.
The meal was terrifying and holy.

Out in mid-Atlantic the solo yachtsman was struck by the
cosmic madness,
forged log-books and positions, boasted of having understood
God's shameful secret, set up the equation of human
existence,
threw himself into the violent spiral of insight and bliss,
until death reached him in the solitary cell
when his imagination ate itself and called for rebirth.

In the empty drifting vessel they found the log-book
and the caricature of a dream, while Ajax
heroically and furiously defeated the flock of sheep.

The Happy Forenoon

He went out. An old frowsty eagle
beginning to lose his plumage.
The sunlight was coarse and offensive.

The day was mild. His body surprised in its tweed coat,
trembling, tired. Innocent and astonished
he saw the sun on the cemetery gravel.
A few children were shrieking.

He hated the lot and most of all
not feeling happy. And the body around him
replied with an unexpected mildness.

As if it didn't care if something in him screamed
for alcohol or love. As if it didn't
know of anything beyond a moment's flicker of sunlight.
As if it didn't know he'd die from the lot:
the children in their overalls, the gravel on the slope, the pale
and patchy skin.
The bones, the muscles, whatever was happy,
guided him where he wanted.

Ezekiel

Can you hear the singing from inside the church?
Who is singing? Cracked voices, old women?
Is someone lying in the coffin? Has it been emptied, plundered?
Is there someone there, dead bones, clothed in sinews,
dead sinews, grown together with muscles, flesh?

In the sand-box a bird with bloody feathers
is covered with tiny flies.
The bacterial process continues.

The hymn falls silent, the stone bleeds.
The prayers chafe against the stone. The voices chafe
against the prayer. The hymn chafes against the stone.

The Twin Sister

The mother reads from a porcelain-white book.
The world has already gone under.

Rain falls. Seven drops. At last.
The twin sister's weeping is just as sudden.

She can't help laughing, living.
She is youth, she has golden skin.

The mother walks over to the bed.
She has already seen everything.
She peels the gold foil from the gleaming shoulder.

Pietà

The boy who was a shoulder-blade, a gold shoulder-blade.
The light coming from him, the hormones of puberty
which were altering his body, were at work in him
whatever his deformity, and the mother who returned
that light to him where he lay behind the cot bars, weak
and drivelling. Was it love? Was it mercy?
She called to him by his name. The name
he didn't hear.

Anemone
For Elsa Rosenquist 1889-1972

The gaze of the dark blue anemone
There is stillness around you
A newborn child cries, its natal fat
round its shoulders
I'm standing by a brick wall, by a telephone

Your voice — the last of it — before your stroke.
This whole hospital is crumbling, the red
brick-cells letting go of each other.
You too were here in its files, so close
to the begonias in the churchyard, the grave with no stone.

It is misty here. What shall I tell you about? The leaking
nuclear power-stations, the new wars, the newborn children?
You have given me a blessing
Twenty years have now passed.
I placed the vase with the blue anemones
on the unsteady table and stooped over
the dark petals, your gaze.

Staffan Söderblom

Translator's Preface

Born in 1944, Staffan Söderblom lives in Kårsta, just north of Stockholm. He has produced nearly twenty books — poems, essays, novels, criticism (most recently, a study of Harry Martinson). He is not prolific as a poet but it is clear that his poetry holds a central place in his writing: short and dense, his poems weigh more than they may at first sight appear to do.

Lennart Sjögren began an essay on Söderblom (*Café Existens* No.44, 1990) like this:

Meeting Söderblom's poetry is like walking into a deep forest in winter... When the snow cascades from a spruce, bewilderment is total, everything that seems clearly articulated in the world of the senses appears suddenly to be mingled with inarticulate signs and secrets.

The factual and the concrete remain factual and concrete in these poems, yet, as Sjögren points out, they are arranged for us in such a way that we abruptly come face to face with precipitous perspectives. Söderblom writes not about nature but from within it: as if 'nature sees him more than he sees nature'. Something of this feeling must have been in Leif Nylén's mind when, reviewing *The Dead Man Breathes* (Dagens Nyheter 01:10:93), he remarked that in his poems:

Söderblom seems not to be walking before us, pointing, but more often to be moving behind the reader's back, coming in from the side or hastily turning away, whispering in the darkness.

Here are two short pieces:

> It was at sea: I woke up.
> The hull scraped along the seabed.
>
> Someone was playing an organ in the engine-room.
> The darkness heavy as two coins.

and

> I don't write the poems.
> I write to order, not the poems.
>
> I write only the poems
> I don't kill off some other way.

The first of these is one section of a set of poems included in *White Territory* (1983). The second is the opening piece of *The Poems* (1987), a gathering of miniatures in which 'the poems', in a remarkable variety of guises, exhibit a remarkable variety of behaviour, usually at odds with 'normal' expectations. The stylistic distance between these two indicates something of the range within which Söderblom has worked. His poems are still very compact, but the earlier ones were almost telegraphic, typographical white space around the brief phrases suggesting the space and time which the reader needed to allow the echoes to flow out and round. In spite of their cryptic manner and an apparently limited landscape in which to operate (often with a lot of snow), the earlier poems are really quite eventful.

More recent poems, stylistically, show a freer hand with line lengths — perhaps 'freer' is wrong if it suggests diminishing control, for the sense of control is indeed heightened. The lines are broken very skilfully. Also in these later poems, with the presence of 'the dead man', we find a new assurance in the exploration of seeming contradictions. Mirror effects ambush us — the future may appear where we expected the past. The factual and the absurd may reflect each other and coexist. Sounds play an important part, and the silence can be so intense that it takes its place among them as a kind of sound on its own. Sounds of course include words: utterance and silence meet at an inexplicable frontier where simple contrasts between them are no longer valid. Doubts about the power of language may be pushed to a limit where they border on faith in the possibilties of language. The reader's feeling of surprise and unease is generated yet held in place by the firmness of the poems. 'The nouns show their strong core,' is how Sjögren put it. 'The poems are there like small hard bodies.'

Thunder: in the Distance

August arrives and the forest
blackens: as in a downpour.

Thunder passes at a distance.
Like huge steamers with shining portholes
along the season.

Something turning its back.

An image from an old-fashioned lecture hall
in the country. The audience.

Rising from their chairs now: staring
at the door.

First Night of the Voyage

1

The anchor goes like a tree
up into the clouds.

The boat tethered for the night: grazes
on the bladder wrack.

Deeper into the sound. They're raising
a hoop net.
The darkness pours through the meshes

out between the islands.

An image gathered from sleep.
It nudges the hull
far below the water-line.

A reef where the channel still breaks.

2

The anchor catches in the seabed stones.
But the journey continues. The boat

ages quickly into an image
from other times: an eider

with one long claw trailing in the depths.

The sun rides bareback in the pines
in the island's interior.

The journey continues and the light lets go
of things. Dream:

Swimming slowly over the sudden
chasms.

Six October Poems

1

Late evening with notes from
an autumnal topography:

territory slowly falling apart.

A black woodpecker crowed all day
and one of the birches went wildly green

for a moment until darkness came
more quickly than a word.

The night is blowing now from the south-east.
The house turns its forehead to the wind.

A piece of the language I belong to
wakens now. With the foxes.

— The scent acrid!

2

October map.
Lakes dark and full-bellied.

Snow-cries in the trees.
They take more time than language.

The crows from the east pass silently over
in the margins of a read-apart text.

Each word murmurs with voices
that take more time than language.

I, along a ditch and a fox-run.
Along the boundary.

3

During the night: a fox ran in the ditch.
Read signs in the new snow! Winter hunger.

Inside the spruce-copse. The crows sunk
each in his chapter of the great story.

I stay indoors. The whole day
stitched through by frontiers to cross. To be
the map that becomes undecipherable.

The cawing of crows: it drifts out over the forest.

4

The turn of the year and sunlight beats in low
like a hawk through the rooms.

A plough of aged light drives through the parish.
The crows whirl out of autumn's chimneys.

It's a wild and happy time.
Down among the animals. Compelled to love.

5

The silence of pinewoods.
It has buzzard's beak and badger's claws. It's there

when the black woodpecker calls. Like a ground-frost
under the cry.

No paths lead into it.

Forwards — or where I stopped.
The words rest in the terrain.

They return along a back-track.
Out of the future.

6

The rain's hooves over the fields.
The house locked up like a loose-box.

I walk the rooms where
an old chilly silence beats
and beats in the walls.

Feeding the invisible cattle.

Nailing Up Eels

Flat-bottomed night
and remote thunder rumbling with the oars.

The house moored in the birchwood

but behind the wallpaper an invisible door
slams.

This may be written :

The outer skerries in June
with open-air paintings from childhood.

The greening watery half-light in the boathouses
and the swallows raising

summer's blue deck planks
still higher over the hard keels.

On the jetty outside someone is nailing up
three eels on the red wooden wall:

rope-ends beating in the wake of the great voyage.

Then a cry falls from the day's windows
from the cloud
and the hill —

a white cry that glides low across the water
out to the stones of the gulls.

This is stronger than grammar
and the Gospels.

This is the silent language
where oblivion finds its alphabets.

And the evenings come. Vapours rise
from the sea. A boat engine chugs across the strait.

This may be written :

Thunder — two seconds between the oar-strokes.
The invisible door slams.

Winter's Margin

1

Winter came.
Not even the birches escaped.
The snow lit childish lamps
on all the graves.

2

The waters are ridden by untamed ice.
Quietly.

3

Here is the well
and the spruce forest arches its back.
Here under the snow

the well's plea.

And deep within the firewood
axe-blows.
Someone filling in an old well.

4

The white word.
It sinks through the text.
A coin in a well.
A stone in the ice.
The wild fathomless ice.

5

The February lake.
The ice is a joiner's bench:
drill-holes and gouge-marks made by sharp iron.

Far out, a black shape.
Nail beneath the sun's
sledge-hammer.

On Grass

The poems finger the scythe and watch the grass.

They stand fingering the scythe,
watching the grass.

They finger the scythe and watch
the grass.

On Birds

The poems are in the bird-book.

Shoes in the bird-book and cap in the clouds.

I read to them: *chaffinch, hoopoe, swallow,
garden warbler*.

I read more.

They are never disappointed.

On Landscape

The poems stride in the map.

They carry a landscape in their coat-pocket,
a home district like a snuff-box in their coat-pocket.

They scrutinize the signs on the map:
the signs for coniferous woods and deserted houses,
the signs for water-mills and bare mountains.

They roam in the map's greenery.

In their coat-pocket they carry the landscape,
the snuff-box and the compass.

On Food

The poems spread butter on their crispbread.

They spread it on the smooth poor-man's side.

Not on account of poverty or solidarity,
nor because of their well-heeled childhood.

On Power

The poems are authorities.

They have telephone-answering machines.

They know nothing of responsibility.

They are obliging.

On Money

The poems give no money.

They *are* money,
not the credit-card sewn into the mattress.

They are the coins that jingle in the trouser-pocket
when the call-box has been vandalized.

On Evening

The poems don't listen to appeals.

They stand by the gate in the evening,
turned to the black foliage.

They stand facing the earthy darkness
that is ploughed by the moon.

They don't listen.

They stand by the gate in the evening,
turned to the sorrow that is called history.

On Nothing

The poems stop short in the face of death.
They are curious.

They push through the funeral guests,
stop short at the hole.

Then clamber down in the hole,
I hear earth and pebbles trickling down.

The poems know nothing about death.

They can't tolerate silence.

All they do is hide,
they hide and all they give is comfort.

On Environment

The poems watch the blowing wind.

They observe the invisible wind
that leafs through the apple-tree.

They watch the invisible sour wind
that lies down on the hill
wrapped in its tail of spruce.

The poems leaf through The Iliad,
it'll soon be finished.

On Time

The poems stand on the platform, freezing.

First comes winter, then the train.

Winter draws in, snow tumbles from the spruces,
a crow sings beneath the clouds.

Winter doesn't stop at the stations.

The train draws in, someone leans out of the window,
throws up and laughs.

The train doesn't stop at the stations.

The poems stand in the timetable, freezing.

On Love

The poems don't want to be written.

They are like the crows I love.

Cawing in the winter daylight
they sacrifice the individual for the species.

On Shoes

The poems count degrees of frost.

They count: minus 4, minus 9, minus 27.

Snow is falling and I'm walking home.

I observe my shoes in the snow,
they're like two crows.

The poems count my steps.

Ornithology

(Six Choruses)

Snow is falling.
I waken in an unoccupied house.
The windows are switched off, daylight passes on.
It's still too soon to write *home*.

🐦

Snow is falling on the birches, the birches exist.
Snow is falling on the birds, the birds exist.

Between the word *birch* and the word *bird* is the wood.
In the wood the word *I* exists.

🐦

Snow is falling on the house where I waken.
The house has four hooves, it's a horse.
The house trots through the nights, it stops in the snow.
It stops near the sky, far from the villages of Sabaoth.

🐦

Snow is falling in my old bootprints.
I stride in my old bootprints in the snow.
I imitate a bright and simple memory.

Snow is falling, the birches are blue.

Snow is falling: music and dense snow.
In the black between the notes death takes the leap.
In the black between the notes is the word *world*, the world.

Snow is falling.
It's the snow falling.
It's the pen reading the words on the paper.
It's the crows dragging the sky through the woods.

I Cut the Dead Man's Logs

1

I cut the dead man's logs,
the slender aspens he got in
before the snow fell and the moon
became a grindstone.

I burn the dead man's clothes,
and the evening bus shines like a parish church,
the driver's
face painted by Albertus Pictor.

I eat the dead man's bread,
to drink: no-man's drink.

2

I burn the dead man's clothes
in the whiteness that is the snow,
the blackness that is the forest.

I am burning his clothes,
the whiteness is sorrow and birch trees,
sorrow and birch trees,
sorrow and a few birches in the blackness
that is the forest.

I cut the dead man's logs,
his shoes are standing in the white snow.

3

I cut the dead man's logs,
the saw doesn't weary, nor do the logs.
Only the words are weary,
on the table where the books lie
and the letters as he left them.
They have spoken silence so long,
eternity can't be measured any longer.
Now they have wearied.
And the forest too, where the logs grow,
has wearied.

4

I eat the dead man's bread, the dead man's
bread, observe the empty snowy fields.

The man walking out there is a figure on a white wall in a
                                         stone church,
he pauses surrounded by skeleton-men and angels with
                                              trumpets,
fingers his empty snowy face
and moves on.

I'm sitting behind the window, feel a hunger,
eat the dead man's bread.

5

I cut the dead man's logs,
fill my pockets with sawdust and dry leaves.

I detest language,
speak non-stop to make language break down,
I cut the alphabet to bits.

I walk backwards in the new snow with my pockets full
of new silence,
backwards
out in the oldest silence.

The Birds

September, late.
The weather described accurately:
the hard sounds of the birds.
Not calls, voices.
Their hard
sounds.

The Shadow of the Trees

I'd rather tell lies.

It's true that the trees have returned from winter,
their shadow falls here,
a coolness darkening in the air here,
the shadow of the trees is like a shower of rain,
memories are all filled like pails with the shadow of the trees,
this is true,
but I'd rather tell lies.

The Word

One day like this
winter day when everything's surrounded by woods
and bristling cold
the word *enemy* comes towards me.
The word *enemy*
becomes as long as the country road I'm walking today.
I walk along the word *enemy*
away towards evening,
towards evening
when the constellations are lit in the snow.
This is where we were coming, too.

The Letter

The letter lying open on the table where I left it,
it's an open space,
a crowd,
their backs towards me,
it's a mass meeting, everyone's listening, standing motionless
                                                                listening
to a speaker I can't see.
Can't hear.

The Water Shines

I step out of the water,
it's evening, the water is shining, I stride up the stairway
of the depths.
Alone here, I am no tree but hear the trees breathing,
and behind my back the man I don't know breaks free,
swims silently
back out in the shining water.

In the Landscape

In the darkness of the landscape.
When the face is no longer visible
the words are visible,
when the words are no longer visible
history is visible.
I see the mountain's face.

I Call the Animals

I call the animals home. They're resting out there
in transparency. I call through the wall with
a hundred portraits hung on it,
each day
a hundred new portraits
are hung on it.
I call the animals home now, the animals, the white
winter animals,
home to the transparent language.

The Forest

The forest has many stairways, few doors, I
walk closer to it, grow older, stand here now
calling
across the water.
It's my voice fluttering among the trees
and the pine-cones on the other side, small and brown-
speckled and big-eyed like a nightjar.
It doesn't come back.
The stones can be seen down
in the water,
few doors.

It was Dark Here

It was dark here last time, I remember the darkness, not
so much more.
I like the kind of poem
that reminds me of bad translations.
Being a bird is not hard,
some days.
It's harder being the site
the bird returns to.

The Unpainted Buildings

The unpainted buildings, places, the un-
painted lives, he thinks to himself
on the way home from
the lake.
The unpainted lake
where I
shall swim
as a dead man, he says
silently to himself, without looking over his shoulder,
without hastening his step. He
passes me, rather: he passes
through me
as we say for lack of a better expression,
each day
on the way home
from the lake where the sandpiper flies six inches
above its mirror-image.

The Dead Man is Poetic

The dead man is poetic. He takes all the time
in the world, he's happy
and relieved
because people are forgetting him so soon. Such
happiness,
such happiness can be answered
only with naivety.
I e.g.
think that these poems I'm writing are
the dead man's laughter.

Not a Living Soul

Not a living soul on this side of darkness. It's
snowing outside, the animals leave their tracks
in the snow.
Small vessels
which the moon fills with blue drink.

It's the Rowan Tree's Work

It's the rowan tree's work today to
bear red berries. See how red the berries are,
she thinks
behind the tree's back.
There are birds flying in every direction and every
cloud, and it's the tree's work
today
to turn its back on her.

The Dead Man Breathes

The dead man breathes. You think about it afterwards. You
think about trees
full of water
and earth.
That's the work of the trees. It's done now. It's
slightly comic, thinking about these poems. When
the poem is done
you
soon forget it.
It has passed into water and earth.

When She Speaks

When she speaks the words are made of wood.
The saw doesn't answer.
The saw
hangs on the nail that doesn't answer her.
The spade has been left in the earth where I dug down to
the dead man.

He's Standing at the Edge

He's standing at the edge ... hard now to
see, he's there at the forest edge, he's turned
this way. They've
caught
up with him now,
and you
can wait in the car for this is a very
old memory.
He walked across open ground,
a field,
stubble,
he walked *carefully*.
He has stopped at the edge of the greenery there. He
is facing this way. You can wait in the car
for now
he's *bellowing* again.

In the Falling

In the falling of the leaves, when the tree empties its baskets
brimful of
yellow leaves,
red leaves ... he sees
transparency again.
In the falling of the leaves,
in the everlasting fall of the leaves from the tree, there is also
a contrary movement. It's
a large
transparent figure slowly,
endlessly slowly
climbing up in the thinning tree-top where
the sky shines in.
That's what he sees.

Slender as a Scream

Slender as a scream, he reaches higher
than the trees now,
he moves with dancing steps in the evening where
the midges are dancing too ... it's midges that
language will look like
when all the words
have decomposed out of it, a weightless
transparent dance.
It's about him I dream,
and about her
when she carries him like an armful
of washing.

He Comes to a Stop

He comes to a stop, turns towards the sharp
light. He was on his way
out of the picture,
now he's regarding the sharp light
attentively,
as if doing a calculation.
She says: We've kept him back here too long
and I think sorrow is
the worst,
sorrow is a detestable way of regarding
him.
He has come to a stop, he's standing now,
restless,
his gaze up towards the sharp light.

Werner Aspenström

Translator's Preface

In a well-known poem called 'Portrait in December' from his 1956 collection *Dikter under träden* (*Poems beneath the Trees*) Werner Aspenström describes himself as 'resident but not at home in' Stockholm. After his upbringing in the heart of rural Sweden (he was born in 1918 in Norrbäcke) he came to Stockholm as a young man, graduated from the university there in 1945, was one of the editors of the literary magazine *40-tal* (*The Forties*) from 1944 to 1947, and stayed on for the rest of his life in the capital, with summer visits to Kymendö (Strindberg's 'Hemsö') in the Stockholm Archipelago. He was an active member of The Swedish Academy from 1981 to 1989. Over the decades his steady output of poems, essays and plays secured him a special place among both 'general' readers and his fellow writers.

Whether or not all this gave him a feeling of being 'at home' in Stockholm I can't say: but the persona which meets us in much of his writing does seem troubled by an incomplete sense of belonging (anywhere?). Certainly the contrast between the way of life he experienced as a child and the way of life surrounding him in modern Stockholm is extreme, but I doubt if biographical facts alone can 'explain' the unease with which he often faced the world.

Here are two poems. The first is one of the so-called fragments (poems, dreams, reminiscences) which make up *Fragmentarium* (1987):

They rowed out to sea
and it was enigmatically deep.
She wondered:
seas are not bottomless are they?
Take that line
and measure!
He leaned out,
saw the sky mingle
with the darkness.
He admitted truly:
I don't dare plummet
that abyss!
Then in her disappointment
she was truly enraged.
They turned, glided towards land
and left their boat.
But the firm land
was no longer firm.
The smooth plain
rose in waves.
And all seas, all seas
were bottomless.

The second is from his 1991 collection.

> *Project*
> Listen for a while to those who cry 'must'.
> Then interrupt.
>
> Listen for a while to those who cry 'no-one must'.
> Then interrupt.
>
> Stand for a while on what is 'our common
>   fundament'.
> Then fall fathomless.

I'm not sure if these are among his best known poems but they are certainly characteristic. We can see, for example, both fascination and terror in the face of the awesome enigmas that surround us. And we can see how this awareness encourages a keen scepticism towards those who claim to understand such mysteries, those who 'know', those who put their trust in grand explanations. Neither art nor nature can cure our anxiety.

In an interview (*Dagens Nyheter* 20:06:69) Aspenström declared that 'the fine arts don't give much support when a depression hits you'. That is the interviewee responding to a journalist and it is one kind of truth. We find another sort if we turn to the essayist: in 'Attempts at Surrealism', collected in *Skäll* (*Causes*) in 1970, he describes a walk across central Stockholm in search of the 'surrealistic' surprise to be found in the chance combination of things seen. The search is in vain and he concludes:

Had I come across anything surreal, had anything happened on the way here to banish my feeling of dumbness? No, that I can truthfully say. It was my own fault, and it doesn't matter. What I am sure of is that Giacometti's secretive 153 centimeter high sculpture will open something that's closed inside me, which the reality outside couldn't do.

At certain periods, on certain days of low pressure, a work of art can be more life-giving than life itself, that is something we can readily admit without humming and hawing ...

In 'Sunflowers in the Dark or, Will Verdure Heal Anxiety?' from *Sommar* (*Summer*), 1968, he speculates on the inadequacy of nature as a source of comfort. A pastoral view of nature means closing our eyes to most of what goes on in nature. 'Yet' — there is always a 'yet' —

Very well, I decide that notwithstanding a night of sleeplessness and nightmares the morning is beautiful, here, now. A silvery haze. A quiet wood. A subdued moon-coloured sun a portent, high rain clouds are watering the eastern half of the sky.

I come down to the water. My shadow frightens and scatters a shoal of fry which had hovered there nosing right into the shore of the shallow reedy inlet. They flee in panic out to deeper water, reunite and return as a thin groping coil, accept my existence so long as I don't move, pack themselves closer, not in a military way but freely darting and nudging into a harmonic throng, a compound organism. No outer enclosure, no central regime, what kind of invisible third power is it that holds together the shoals, the swarms, the herds and the nebulae? I watch their fellowship with envy.

Whether he is recalling his childhood from a lost society or watching animals today or looking at pictures or trying to write down his dreams, Aspenström the poet constantly surprises us with his ingenious ways of revealing large issues by looking at small and apparently marginal items or events, and of somehow giving us a sense of a life-enhancing view even when that view contains very bleak perspectives. He may never have become street-wise in an urban sense but he certainly retained a countryman's sense of the immediacy of humble and practical objects and of the adjacent but alien lives of beasts, whether of more or less domestic cats, of the cattle on a farm, or of 'wild' sparrows.

When Wisława Szymborska was given the Nobel Prize for Literature in the autumn of 1996 a Swedish commentator pointed out, rightly, that the closest equivalent in Swedish poetry to her ingenious form of ironic regard is to be found in Aspenström. Aspenström had himself declared his sense of affinity with the Polish poet in his poem to and about Szymborska: it was collected in his 1993 volume and I have included it here. He refers to Szymborska as 'she from Poland'.

The wry tone of Aspenström's poems disarms the reader, in more than one sense. It is a tone which *seems* to survive the language barrier but that seeming could be deceptive. Puns and allusions have to stay behind in the original language, where they belong, and their resistance to translation is in a way unproblematic. Less obvious to the reader of Aspenström in translation perhaps is the fact — which is one of the features that make him attractive to Swedish readers — that this wry tone is combined with a musicality which belongs, of course, entirely to his native Swedish.

From *The Red Cloud*

[*Det röda molnet* / *The Red Cloud* (Bonniers, Stockholm, 1986) is a collage of poems, transcribed dreams (some of them quoted from 'The Black Books', a depository covering thirty-five years), recollections of childhood scenes, and accounts of everyday events whose reality may well seem less vivid than the events of dreams and less urgent than the memories of people and things which no longer exist.]

In the dream a red cloud had anchored itself above the white cross on top of the parish church. I was standing quite far away. What year it was I don't remember, it was in the 1920s. I was in one of the lower classes at the local school. I felt obscurely that the intensely glowing cloud had some intention towards me, I didn't brood over the matter for long. The same nocturnal sight returned a couple of times, was erased and forgotten, only to turn up again as an incandescent memory in my adult space-dreams.

The Tree

I remember a tree, a maple, a maple-dome
that autumn had for long been eyeing.
I remember when its crown in near-silence fell
and settled like a wreath round its foot.
A peaceful country road, I remember,
drew past.
There had been war
and never more would be.
The boy from the next farm came and bathed
in the maple's lake.
We pledged each other that we'd never
or not until we're very old, die.
A magpie was sitting on a fence-post
laughing
as not just magpies do.

ế ế ế

The gates have been unhooked, the stone posts lean, the huge
maple-roots are pushing. If you stand in the hole which was the
gateway and look up at the timber building at the top of the
slope you can imagine it is an ark gone aground and aban-
doned.

To see it this way you have to know it is a barn you are
looking at, that animals were once lodged inside it. Now the
three stalls are empty, the sty is empty, the pen is empty, and

so is the little gallery above the pen, where the hens had their winter quarters. They weren't let out until May. The wide-meshed wire-netting, which was kept in a big roll, would be wound out and secured on stakes hammered into the ground. After the preliminary period of wandering around and test-scratching and being surprised at the greater freedom they would get down to digging for worms, as febrile as newly-arrived prospectors in the Klondike.

What had once been an enclosed lawn in front of the barn ran the length of the building and was trampled by hooves, now the grass grows there quite undisturbed. The path turns off towards the shed full of neatly stacked firewood. The fence has collapsed, on the photograph in front of me it is still upright. Inside the high gate that leads out to the forest two cows pose, both with horns, the one red and white, the other dappled, the latter with the rank of bell-cow. The bell was of metal and probably home-made, like most of the wooden and iron objects on the farm. The red and white cow is staring into the camera bellows. Her gaze we can say is inscrutable. In front of the bell-cow stands the girl who has milked them and who will now take them out to pasture in the woods. She is wearing an ankle-length dress, and over that an apron that reaches almost to the hem of her dress, and over that again a cardigan of the kind that tends to sag in front and hang awry.

A placid picture, filled with the peace of the inaccessible, everything is visible but concluded, over and done with. The fence has done its job and is gone, the forest path has done its job. Of the milkmaid there is only a skeleton, buried and tumbled in with the remnants of kith and kin in the family grave. Of the horned cattle there is perhaps not as much as a flake of the four horns. The photographer is finished with picture-taking and lies bedded-down in a grave in another parish. Recollections of bustle and noise magnify the echo when you return to an abandoned house. The ark reverberates. If I entered one of the stalls, put the halter round my own neck and shook and rattled as hard as I could, the silence would not be expelled, it would grow.

What's over and done with is nothing to mourn about or conjure melancholy out of. The masters of the farms die, their animals are taken to the slaughter.

ዮ ዮ ዮ

'Probably a long overcoat, a surtout of some stiff material, a bluish-black fabric with flecks of gold, it stood rock-still on the sea, an ocean without waves. The lower edge of the coat followed the surface of the water, no feet protruded. Above, it vanished with its collar into the clouds, no face could be distinguished, the neck opening was empty. Yet there was no doubt that a mighty owner found himself inside the coat, which was supplied with more buttons than button-holes, the buttons were spread over the front and varied in size. Some were firmly attached, others dangled on fragile threads, some fell — not abruptly like shooting stars but drifting down as if they hung from parachutes.

While I lay there in bed speculating over what I had seen and thinking I had found certain correspondences between ourselves and the buttons, the bells in St Mary's Church began ringing, we live at the same height as the bells. School term ended that day. The pupils had already been to their classrooms to fetch their marks. Listening to the clamour I couldn't decide if all three bells were at work, likely just two. The feeling of being a dangling button stayed with me all morning.'

🔔🔔🔔

We too are Laymen, said the Waves

Two nights in a row setting out from Stavanger
I made my way on foot over the Atlantic
between icebergs and oil-rigs
to the accompaniment
of excited conversations with the waves
who comforted me saying:
'We too are laymen.'

A feeble daylight memory and a lively nocturnal dream-life go together, I have a theory about that. Those of us with weak memories have undermanned border patrols, phantoms and things that shun the light easily slip through. How we envy those blessed with contours, those born with clear demarcation lines in their souls! As a means of counteracting haziness I got myself some notebooks, covered in black oil-cloth, and I filled them with things I copied down, press-cuttings, news-items, facts, suggestions, bright ideas. A mistake. I should have taken a lesson from the squirrel who digs down his nuts and forgets where. I often think I know that something I need lies hidden in the black pile. I just don't know in which volume and I give up. Now when I browse through them, I'm surprised by how numerous these written-down dreams are, how interlocked they are, and how dreamlike seems much of what we classify as realities and facts.

Dreamlike. 'Just before midnight at the end of an eventful day we walk through the enclosure down to the shore to look out across the surface and listen to the dying wave-beats, our impressions of the day have calmed down, out here the air is quite still. No lit window among the cottages on the islets over there, no mast-head lanterns on a boat, no moon. Of the pale stars only one is shining brightly and that is no star but a planet, Jupiter. It is gleaming so brightly that it sends a shimmering pathway over the strait. It leads to another shining point on the flat rock of the shore, a glow-worm. How good to meet again, and it must be ages since last time! But it's madness to lie here, on this cold bedrock, unprotected and only a metre away from the water's edge! Yet there it lies, shining not quite like Jupiter but nonetheless twinkling in its own manner. We stand there for a while and try in vain to hit upon a suitable word for the listless, not clucking yet muttering sound of the waves meeting the stones, dividing, folding into each other and in sleepy embraces dying away. After a time one of those modern man-made stars reveals itself in the south-west sky, it *crosses* the beams from Jupiter and vanishes north-eastwards. There remain the two phenomena not made by man, a glow-worm and a planet. Our position is such that the line of light from them runs straight as a ruler into our eyes.'

Not a dream at all but something which ought to have been the opposite of a dream yet wasn't — a perfectly uneventful walk in a 'real' winter landscape:

'Observed and collected: three horses, two biggish and one a pony. A hare. A few crows. My companions caught up with me and told me they'd seen a big blood-stain, which led their thoughts to murder and other disagreeable things with which the newspapers had recently been frightening us. I took off down a side-road. Through a half-open barn door I caught sight of some cows and a gold-coloured tap, probably it was bronze. A couple of girls at the giggling age were busy inside. I called them out and asked the best way down to the water, an ice-bound corner of Lake Mälar. Inland plain, long alley, shuttered summer cottages with everlasting flowers in the windows. The snow crunched. The crust held only children, grown-ups stepped through it.'

If dream images are simply distorted reflections of things we have previously seen and been affected by, then the enemy squadrons which most recently showed themselves in the air-space above a village in Southern Dalarna should have been German and the landscape that around Mecklenburg. In the summer of 1939 my intention was to make my way to Berlin, either on foot or by hitch-hiking, but I never reached Berlin and I still haven't. One evening I had lain down on the ground to sleep in a half-grown pine plantation outside Rostock. Twice I was wakened, first by a wild animal which studied me in a curious but friendly manner, like the calves of childhood, and then by a formation of Messerschmidts practising for the imminent attack on Poland.

One of the Horse's Legs was Missing

Well-groomed but with glassy stare
an Ardennes horse stood
among the hazel-bushes in the pasture.
One of the horse's legs was missing.

Under the horse lay a man in a white coat,
a vet perhaps or a taxidermist.
Slowly another of the horse's legs gave way.
I saw, I foresaw, I didn't interfere.

Untouched I watched what happened: how the giant
tottered and fell and threatened to crush the man.
I was the only witness in the beautiful pasture,
that beautiful, not unfamiliar pasture

where in certain summers hazel-nuts could be plucked
and a family of lynxes was recently seen,
those splendidly supple and shy creatures
who slink between waking and dream.

Not a dream but a simple occurrence in Stockholm.
'The clock tower had just begun its twelve strokes as I was
passing the end of a lane. The sunlight poured right down in
the cleft between the house walls, my mood matched the
weather. While the clock proceeded with its counting, a
window on the third storey suddenly opened, a woman leaned

out to shake a cloth or shawl and it slipped out of her fingers. The scrap of fabric, red in itself, glowed even more brightly in the noon sun and sailed like a flaming torch down to the shadowy pavement, where the sun never reaches. In the year 1759, in the same month as this, 250 houses were destroyed by a fire which the telepathic Swedenborg saw from a distance of 300 miles. The blaze lasted for 24 hours. On this summer day everything was over in 10 seconds.'

The Cat Pricks up its Ears

The striped cat pricks up its ears.
The striped cat jumps down from the bed.
The black stripes slink towards the door.

The pricked-up ears hear steps on the stairway.
The dilated pupils see someone coming.
The black stripes arch their back.

My dilated brain knows no-one is coming.
My intelligence is incontestable, the other night
I played chess with Voltaire — and won.

The theories about ghosts have never been confirmed.
The bats in Transsylvania don't suck blood.
I'm still lying calmly in bed, trembling.

One morning I take my place on a north-bound train in order to return and inspect the nocturnal outposts.

There's a great silence in emptied houses, but now and then you can hear a click and at isolated points in the general sound-lessness you can hear a noise like fine rain, a faint rustling. In the summer there might be a bang like a shotgun as the morning sun pushes into the house and heats up and expands a metal can or empty cask. Towards evening there might be another bang as the metal cools and contracts. Desolate but not entirely deserted. Those of high stature rearrange their lives or depart, the human beings, and with them the cattle vanish. Those of small stature stay on, or move in and make themselves at home. The mice nibble, the spiders tie their nets, the beetles drill their way in and leave tiny heaps of sawdust behind them. Swallows flutter in, rip the cobwebs, whirl up the chaff and dust.

The roof-ridge sags, the walls bulge, the timber beams sink with their own weight, the filling between them flattens out like worn cartilage, the wooden pegs dry and creep out of their holes, the long split-pins are certainly tough but in the long run they can't hold out against the rust. The corner-stones are pressed down into the earth, unevenly. The building begins to crouch like an old person.

The main barn is of solid timber, the extension is boarded. On the upper floor of this extension is the threshing machine, most of whose parts were devised and made by my grand-father, a versatile but according to witnesses gruff-natured fellow. Both for himself and for others he put up robust con-structions which stood up to the transition from 'tramping', i.e. horse-power in a literal sense, to the application of electricity, in spite of the lack of subtleties like ball-bearings. The journals rested on cast-iron bearings, sticky with the quantities of heavy-duty oil with which they had to be nourished.

Equipped with camera and flash I come to the threshing machine with a purpose, I want to make sure of the colour of the drum. Was it pure blue, or more, as I believe, bluish-green? Or have I remembered quite wrongly, was it unpainted? Why is it so important to know the colour of the threshing drum into which the oat-sheaves were once fed? For me it's part of a process of self-defence, it will serve as a protection against the vague, the misty, the floating, it will be a check, something with the stamp of factuality. I want to be able to report the colour exactly, to point it out on Becker's scale.

Many clouds were drifting on the parish sky that day sixty years ago, bright and dark, cirrus and cumulus, many followed their course over the church spire, one of them was red and chose to stop, more or less held to the point, preached something to me which I was not mature enough to grasp. Perhaps it wanted to impress upon me that each one of us in his allotted place is obliged to live attentively and contribute to giving the world a clear outline, to paint, as Diderot put it, 'the works of creation: the birds as well as the nuances of their plumage.' Did the cloud have a suspicion that I would come to break that commandment and fall for the siren's song of melancholy? If I could now determine quite precisely the colour of the thresher's drum then perhaps the nocturnal attacks might stop. To those on the outside this way of thinking may appear absurd. I am not on the outside.

First I stop in front of the big barn, whose timbers are dove-tailed at the corners, and I study the Roman figures hacked by axe-strokes in the beams, eleven in all. Sometimes people would travel into the forest and put up the timber-houses in the same place where they cut the trees, then dismantle them and transport them to the prepared site. The nine is drawn not with a one before the ten, but with four ones after the five, possibly a simpler way to write with an axe. There's something peculiar about the mark in front of the figures, a capital B back to front, which ought to indicate which of the four walls those beams belonged. Why back to front? If I read the whole series backwards then the numbering doesn't fit, the Roman five doesn't tolerate being stood on its head. The solution could be that the man with the axe went over to the opposite side of the pile of prepared and transported beams before cutting the numbers.

I carry on, into the dusky extension, or rather it is streaked with light, the sun cuts into the cracks between the edge-to-edge planks and slices up the darkness. A play of light like that stops us in our tracks, we forget ourselves and our errands. The monks in Ceylon called it *kasina* and assigned various methods. If you are immersing yourself in it you can fix your gaze on a speck of dust or a bowl of water, gaze at a fire through the hole in a piece of cloth, watch how a tree-top moves in the wind and how light seeps through the foliage. This they would have called a *barn-kasina*.

I don't intend to be stopped in my tracks. It's the threshing-machine that is my errand. For two days it would work hard, for the rest of the year it would be lazy, or meditate like the monks of Ceylon. Now it has stood still for several decades. Once I'm up there I find that a 'winnowing-machine', an unwieldy hand-driven device, has been dumped on top of the feeding-board and drum. This gadget was supposed to complete

the threshing process and decisively separate the chaff from the grain. It's too heavy for me to shift on my own.
The exact colour? There is no way I can find out, this time. I ought to be disappointed, but I'm not, particularly. Back down on the floor of the barn I give myself time to scrutinize the thin slices of light in the dusk, and then I return to the main barn and contemplate the three empty stalls and run my hand over the handle of the pump. It has locked itself fast. Water, in any case, can't be expected.

At the Opera I Remember another Song

In tune, with the knife in his breast
Othello *bel canto*'s his way towards death.
Ringing true, Desdemona articulates her song.
The widow, in the gloom of the byre
toiling the milk from the cow's teats,
sang quite beautifully, she too
behind the runnel for manure.

All mothers will sing quite beautifully
for lambs and calves,
for kids and chicks, for piglets
sticking their snouts between the bars
— never full-up with love
which is so big
yet never enough.

We waken convinced that someone is standing breathing behind the closed door. The door-handle turns slowly downwards, the door is not thrown wide open, on the contrary it opens a mere crack, wide enough to let a hand slide in, through the half-darkness you can see the cuff of a blouse or shirt, the tip of a foot may be visible, never a face. Once I saw the hand reach further in and grasp the handle from the inside, as if it thought of closing the door from the inside. Quite unreasonable — the arm's in the way! Magritte joked like this in his pictures, *but in dreams the pictures are breathing*, that is something Magritte could not imitate.

Who is fingering the door-handle and requesting an audience? Could it be others than those who were closest to us and who could not or never managed to say what they wanted — or who did say, and we didn't listen?

In the Age of the Long Exposures

Not like mountains, our fathers,
not like oceans, our mothers,
we can hold them in a cupped hand.
Their rigid troubled stares
try to catch our eyes,
we, not yet born.
Below them, in silver curls,
the name of the studio-owner
who forced them to stand so still
that the fate of us all shows through
under the smooth cheeks.

Livestock can't be left to fend for themselves, in spite of sorrow and distress. Between tasks in the barn she runs down the slope and into the kitchen to squeeze milk for the new-born from her own breast just as she has been squeezing milk from the udders of the cows. Distress was such a large part of life that the addition of yet another death, that of an ailing infant, hardly meant much for the present but relieved the future. (Not to give up the spirit, a debt to be paid off by instalments?) First, the versatile miller, carpenter, threshing-machine builder had been laid in a coffin, which he had quite likely nailed together himself, an implacable old fellow with his wreath-like beard sticking up above the edge of the coffin, but still a parent. Two days later a boy not a year old, an emergency baptism, his fontanel chose not to grow together. The year after that the breadwinner himself, never before sick, famous for his strength, now brought down by the raging epidemic. When the man is carried out to be taken away to the hospital he asks how the sickly new infant is, in his feverish confusion he mixes names and uses the name of a boy on the neighbouring farm. That was the name which the surviving child came to choose for himself.

Elaborate poem or 'I exist' — the message chipped with a pocket-knife, signs and scribbles of life. He who died had a mania for carving his name everywhere he worked, someone tells me. Such proof of his having existed I never found, on the walls of sheds or barns. Just hearsay. One very snowy winter a pair of girls are on their way to school. He is standing on top of a huge pile of snow he has shovelled up, cups his hands round his eyes and says: 'I can see Australia from here.' They believe him, they haven't after all got that far in the geography book. That could indicate a sense of humour, a penchant for the absurd. Next time someone asks me who I really am I shall try to answer: humorist with impediments.

She who Paused on the Path and Breathed Deeply

Dreamt she was not, but in the guise of dream
the water-carrier, shoes half off half on,
she paused and drew a breath so deep
the tree-tops bent towards her,
even the stiff juniper bushes,
and the cloud caravans hesitated in their course.
Underground streams quickly replaced the water
stolen from the well.
Nature,
momentarily disturbed by the sigh of a middle-aged woman,
resumed its dominion.
Dreamt she was not, but in the guise of dream.

Prematurely aged, not so very old in years, she who sat on the milking stool and sadly hummed or half-talked to herself, now it was her turn. I visit her in 'the home', where she has been placed and where she shares a room with a restless insomniac woman. As a child her husband had been in the same establishment for a time with his mother, that was where girls who had 'got into trouble' were sent. She has one last wish that she stammers out: to see the mill-pond again, which had long ago given her, the miller's daughter, hours of happiness. That was out of the question. But I myself, who had begun to write down descriptions of things, could have cycled out there and studied the pond carefully and tried to capture and transmit it with the help of words and likenesses and returned to the sick-room. Not that my image of the pond could replace 'the real' one, the one filed away in her memory, it would have been better than nothing, a kind of applied poetry, in the long run possibly the only kind which can be excused. I didn't go, as likely as not I didn't want to waste time. And afterwards was too late ..

I seldom heard working people in the country recounting dreams they'd had during the night. Was that because they were never frightened by nightmares and didn't dream the normal quota of one and a half hours which the researchers have proved is allocated to us? Is the telling of dreams among us a luxury occupation, part of our manic self-absorption — in contrast to what it is among 'nature' peoples? No doubt they dreamed their ration of dreams, no doubt they allowed themselves day-dreams as well, which were never revealed to anyone, unless they had to do with winning a fortune. Dreams, fancies, sunsets, moonlight, water-lilies, melodies and beautiful words, all that wasn't real reality. What did real reality consist of? Axe, saw, sledge, work-horse. Even so, many finished up beside the water-lily.

The Path of the Strong and Lonely Fellows

Often in lady-loveliest July,
pinched in their leather waistcoats,
they followed the meadow-sweet-edged winter-path
down to the blackest tarn,
where their cycles would be found,
set leaning against peasant-forest spruces.

☙ ☙ ☙

If I could choose a thousand times over I would prefer a strong memory rather than a profusion of dreams. If your memory is feeble you can't even mend an alarm-clock of the older uncomplicated sort, you can take it to bits, not put it together again. But you can train yourself, say brisk friends. Wide awake and sleepless I decide to reconstruct the old long-since disused dairy, where milk from our village and from the next village was delivered and where cheeses were made. Cheeses! Real cheeses! Solid matter!

In the corner over there to the left stood the steam-engine, hungry for wood and slow to get going in the mornings, a good time would pass before it was so hot it would begin to puff and hiss and the connecting rods sighingly set themselves in motion. High up I can make out the centrifuge regulator with its brassy gleam and perpetual spinning, alternating between the two positions 'arms up' and 'arms down'. From the steam-engine power was conveyed to the axle just beneath the roof and then by way of belt-drives down to the separator and the churn on the floor. The leather belts swayed, now and then

169

they would slip off and could not be replaced without trouble. Against the long wall to the right stood a warmed vat where the milk would run and be transformed into cheese. Two young women stirred it with spades which looked like paddles, stirred and stirred until the liquid thickened and set and could be squeezed to a white dripping ball that smelled fresh and tingling and dairy-rousseau-ish. The door at the further end led out to a cold room, where lumps of ice bumped around among the milk-bottles in oblong, iron-bound wooden tubs. The ice, smashed into pieces with a wooden club, was fetched from a crusher outside the cold room. Through a door on the left, on this side of the steam-engine, was a cool cheese store. Wrapped in linen cloths they lay there in long rows on sagging planks, sweating and biding their time. Now and then they had to be turned, as one turns infants, some were corsetted in rigid forms.

Outside the dairy, by the stone base on the left, I think my memory lets me see a waste-pipe, curving down into the earth and leading out to a ditch. If you scratched about in the sand beside the pipe you could find copper coins, mostly one öre and two öre pieces.

Or could you?

I phone my sister, who has a good memory, and ask her. No, she doesn't know anything about that. Are these copper coins also dreamt up? Too bad if they are.

But cheeses! Real cheeses! Solid matter!

Seen from the Balloon of Dreams

A dwarf fire flickered weakly
at the centre of a round field ...
Everything looks circular,
seems slender,
seen from the balloon of dreams ...
Two greatly reduced humans
I thought I recognized
were skiing along the blue
plate-edge ...
Soon the dog's yelping
could no longer be heard ...

Time perhaps to be lifted up?
But I don't want to be lifted up
quite now, quite now
from those down there ...

Freud separated dreams into the latent and the manifest, the obscurity of the lower levels and the distorted images of the surface levels. Long before him, Baudelaire made a similar distinction, calling the first type hieroglyphic, he thought they made up an encyclopedia which ought to be studied. In a more concrete manner than Baudelaire had in mind, this hieroglyphic world was made visible to me. In a dream I saw these Egyptian signs, which the Greeks called 'holy inscriptions', covering the sky above my childhood home, right down to the forest edge. Perhaps at the edges there was an element of cuneiform, which in its turn could possibly have been a continuation of or a reflection from the outspread upper branches of the conifers, they too engrave with a sharp point.

Unlike most messages from space the dream was not frightening, but evinced a sense of happiness similar to what we might feel before a work of art, when the picture seems to be 'ready' and everything in it has fallen into its place, right out to the frame, when a piece of music is written down, to the last chord, when a poem has reached the last definitive line — and thus has freed itself from its begetter and become something autonomous. (Dreams and works of art appear to share this wish to be cut loose from their umbilical ties, to be independent. Can a nightmare then be explained as our punishment for hindering the headstrong dream from coming into existence and developing?) The hieroglyphic heaven was complete, at least this part of it was, the part above the barn, the potato patch and the oat-field.

'Dreamt that two men in formal dress were gathering hay off the drying wires at home, down from the barn. They were quarrelling about some political question, I had the impression one was a communist, the other a social democrat. The row turned to blows. In spite of summer and daylight there appeared along the forest edge a flickering aurora borealis, close to the ground, billowing like the lower hem of a curtain. A hazy multitude separated itself from the glimmer, came close, streamed past. They were of a green substance, a thin, initially transparent matter, a green powder, grass-creatures, leafy beings. They condensed into humans, human faces, faintly brown or pink. They streamed past innumerably from the forest in the north, over the hay-field, to the forest in the south. There was nothing frightening about them, they seemed happy, liberated, light, humans wandering in blessed weightlessness. I spoke to a woman, she was not like anyone I know. Without chiding me, and indeed cheerfully, she let me understand that I should not speak to them, whoever was spoken to would die. At the same moment she changed. Her shimmering green brothers and sisters continued their flight untouched, evaporated in the forest to the south. In her new condition she looked like an enamelled doll or a little porcelain statuette. The face gilded and with one big formless eye.'

☙ ☙ ☙

'In the evening a long conversation with some friends about earthly and heavenly matters and human feelings. Then a walk on a narrow dark lane between half-ripe grain-fields. Clouds, unfortunately, obscure the sky, otherwise we'd have seen several falling stars, which are very common on these first days of August. It's time to lie down, time to sleep, time to dream and it's not long before I find myself once more out on the road and this time beneath a dome of sky higher and mightier than the 'real one'. The stars fluctuate between yellow and orange, they are preternaturally large, like van Gogh's, and arranged in new constellations. Earlier in the evening we'd amused ourselves with the old game of counting how many sounds each of us could distinguish, they were few and faint: crickets, raindrops, rustling leaves, distant cars. The more loudly it thundered in the dream, then, when a boulder huge as a barn broke free of the mountainside and began tumbling after us down on the roadway. The laws of nature were suspended, the boulder did not let itself be hindered by the steep upward slope and it didn't pause until it had reached the crown of the hill and then, without the help of mouth and lips, it began to address us in an authoritative Old Testament style. The number three was mentioned. The drift of its obscure sermon seemed to be that we should not presume to express ourselves on matters beyond our understanding. (The boulder: the cloud, having happened to change its colour and substance?) Woke up in great discomfort.'

There were other things sticking up which the cloud could have fastened itself to, chimneys, look-out towers, eye-catching solitary trees. It could have come to rest above the dim mirror of a forest pond. That it chose to ally itself with the church spire need not signify anything other than the fact that the spire happened to be highest ...

She Thinks It's a Star

The lady with the lilies-of-the-valley is late.
The gates are closed at sunset.
Not clear whom she thinks of visiting:
one of the elevated geniuses
or the rustic one with the taste of earth in his mouth.
Here they lie scattered
those who scattered words.
All light is borrowed.
The planets revolve in fettered orbits
round the sun.
The on-duty mirror just now is Jupiter,
soon to appear on the left of the church tower.
She thinks it's a star,
The bat and the lady with the lilies-of-the-valley
both cry out as they meet beneath the limes.
That they are related
is something she will not believe.

Arch

Lace-up sandals are more beautiful than top-boots
and military museums.
The most beautiful construction, a naked foot.

Churches and town-halls in romanesque style
envy the foot's arch.

Finest of all, the earth's curvature
seen from a headland, out in the sea.

Language

Not only the classic striding on his metric feet,
not only the up-to-date trouble-maker ...

The sea's nerves too, even the waves write poems.
Elegiacally or in full storm they describe the shore
they have in sight and against which they will be crushed.

Of course there are stories outside language.
Pebbles clattering out words.
Foam the phrase-monger.

Soon the Century will Fold its Newspaper

At last — they've gone!
The coat-hangers in the porch sway like gondolas.
Out on the street the quarrel continues
between the meat-eater and the green man.
Who can live safely in the body's cabin?
Mayakovsky, terrified of bacilli,
a soap-box always in his pocket,
was poisoned by love.
In its twenty-third week the embryo starts dreaming.
What can an embryo dream about?
About everything. About incomplete things.
The carp swims dreamlessly
in the century's dwindling pool.

Friends and Relatives

I notice that my mania for truth
has given way to an interest in similarities.
I'm sitting in the back yard of a city tenement
together with three biological friends,
two all black and one striped.
They don't know we are related.
My two comparing pupils observe
six wide-open eyes whose upward stare is fixed
on a square of sky framed by guttering
and this moment traversed by a winged creature
— which is expected to return.

I recognize the stiff bearing of Seekers
on their prominent places in spiritual cafés,
of Sign Interpreters convinced that the veil
will soon be torn,
the zeal of Readers of primary sources.
Someone plunges into Hebrew
to take up again the trial of a God
already condemned to death,
someone else goes for Sumerian
hoping to rediscover the road to Dilmun,
the eternal kingdom of wafting foliage
where the raven doesn't croak,
the lion doesn't kill,
the dove doesn't hang its head
and an old man never says
'I'm an old man'
and his equally old wife never says
'I'm an old woman.'
Dilmun, where laments are never heard.
If only we were there!
The winged creature after resting a while
on the TV mast again crosses
our section of the heavenly dome.
The six wide-open eyes narrow somewhat
and turn their attention to a beetle
who terrified for its life
gallops into its stable between two bricks.

The Stranger

Brotherhood, jostled together in buses on twisting roads
or on ferries in a gathering storm.
Sisterhood, the dread of cancer in waiting rooms
with art-club prints and yellow creepers.
What an unpleasant sort — him, over there,
no need of consolation or illusions.
The shivering pigeons in the square outside
neither touch nor disturb him.
Twice I've asked him who he is
without getting an answer.
You'd think he belonged to some other branch of the
                                        language-tree
or was only a shadow
with the indolence typical of shadows.

In Ten Thousand Years

In ten thousand years the ice will melt.
The frozen-in child will come loose
and take up his game again:
making out of twigs and pine cones
bull, cow and calf
and a fence against death.

The Sun by Night

In the neon cities people are still on the run.
Just now they're streaming out of the cinemas
and vanishing humming in the alleys.

Up here a village lies snoring
with its knees drawn up like an embryo.

The corner lamps are out. But a green moon
shines in the eyes of the night-shift foxes.

If my memory were better I would — for the coffee-pot
and for the spider, who are sleepless too —
stand and declaim Echnaton's hymn to the sun.

Elegy

Because the day wears out.
The sun will die at seven o'clock.
Tell me, expert in darkness,
who will shine over us now?
Who will switch on illumination of a western sort,
who will dream dreams of an eastern sort?

Come — anyone — with a torch!
Preferably you.

My Greek World View

There was nothing in *The Bergslag Post*
about the earthquakes in Japan
that had laid the capital in ruins.
Two women sat in a kitchen
slurping coffee out of saucers
and sighing over their own fates:
one a widow with several children,
one an unmarried girl
who'd done time in a reformatory
for hiding a newborn boy in the marsh.
She had a bad limp.
It was before the age of hip operations.
The Nobel Prize was now being handed out
for discoveries about the atom's interior.

What I could see and hear through the window
confirmed the Greeks' theory of the four elements.
Fire burned in the blacksmith's across the road.
The smith hammered at runners for a timber sledge.
A cart rattled past loaded with earth.
As for the air, it shimmered in the blue
ready to bear everything that wanted to be borne.
From the pond the red-throated diver would return
to the Caspian Sea.
Perhaps above the moon there was a fifth element
supervising the others.

Movements were of two kinds,
one going up and one going down.
They took it in turns endlessly, like gladness and gloom,
like desire and disgust, like the sparks
when the smith pulled the bellows.

They blossomed on their way up from the hearth
and withered on their way down
and blossomed up again
just as the old Greeks had said they would.

The State of Things

Still not night? Winter not yet?
Silence not total? Dreams still flickering?

Warning stickers on everything sent,
everything received: FRAGILE.

Still a great risk of everything breaking
being swept off by whirlwinds

as in Russian folk tales.

If She from Poland Were Here Just Now

If she from Poland were here just now
we could talk about the stones
and their relatives.
Inaccessible, she would complain,
don't open when we knock.
Sometimes! I would then object.
The first stone thrown at Orpheus
fell at his feet, moved by his song.
Then?
Deaf — the second stone was deaf.
The third?
Coloured by blood.
Oh, these escalations!

Nightfall.
Sphinx moths and owlet moths get ready.
The peacock butterfly wanders frozen home from the
                                        blackberry thicket
to the after-warmth of a south-facing wall.
The bat wakens punctually.
A badger shakes off the dust
and trots out on a snail hunt.
In the darkness white flowers begin to give off their
                                        fragrance.

Absurd, stacking up word on word to make twilight poems.
More absurd, not to?
Most happy when the stacks collapse?

We could scrutinize our lists of questions,
if she from Poland were here.
To be human, quite good still?
To be able to grasp something with our thought,
to be able like Dürer to seize a hare
with a brush?
Better to be goshawk, sparrowhawk, marsh harrier, buzzard,
grasp with our claw?

Sit alone, pretty bad?
Two better?
Still better: be many, many, many,
sit packed in assemblies
eat mass-cooked soup?
Better: dream up a spoon
that'll give our soup some taste?

Unborn best?
Unborn not best!
But watch over us, 'swallow-heart!'

I see the blue queen
in the constellation of Lyra.
In Poland it's been visible for long.

Lights going on in the neighbour's.
The privet moth rushes over
thumps against the window panes
wanting in

like song into stone
as everything wants into something else
in our separate kingdoms.

[Note: 'swallow-heart' alludes to a line in a poem by Wisława
Szymborska, the lady from Poland who is the subject of this poem.]

The Girl and the Spider

The father's way of folding the newspaper
reveals his unease at the state of the world.
By clattering in the sink the mother
tries to silence her own thoughts.
Who will look after the girl
who can't sleep?
A spider looks after the girl
who can't sleep,
scuttles down and swings like a pendulum
before her — until she rocks
her lonely head in time
into the little, the friendly death.

The Childish Question

A childish question crops up once again:
where did the quenched flame go,
where did it run in its yellow dress
followed by shadows?
Nothing is annihilated, quite, it only changes place.
The wind crouches and rests for a while
on its way to different weather.
Myself, I cross a churchyard
on my way to the tube station.
Bewailed by black cast-iron tears,
mourned by wife and two children,
here rests power-broker Otto Herman Pauli,
dead 1852.
April now, seven years to the next century.
The ground frost has left the ground.
If annihilation didn't exist
I should feel through the thin soles of my sandals
how the dead breathe.
To avoid breach of duty
the preacher next Sunday will repeat
that Someone 'indeed rose.'
In his glass cage halfway to heaven
the crane operator has a wider view than we have.
With his long arm he piles flat upon flat.
By autumn the whole block will be ready.

Further on, when the wallpapers have faded,
the childish question will crop up again:
where did the quenched flame go,
where did it run in its yellow dress
followed by warm shadows?

The Dream about the Giant Ice-Cube

Not just remote farms but entire villages,
indeed a county town with town hall and cathedral
lay frozen inside the giant ice cube.
I won't forget that dream quickly.
Visible but sealed in, everyday life went its way.
Noises which normally carry long distances,
the howling of chained dogs in the countryside,
screams and laughter from school yards and funfairs in towns,
thumping pile-drivers ... Nothing could be heard.
Whistle in mouth the train guard moved
from carriage to carriage slamming the doors.
As if in a silent film the train rolled off gently.
Untouched by the ice low-voiced flames burned.
Otherwise it can sound like pistol shots
when wood fires crackle and sparks hop out.
What surprised me most was the absolute clarity.
The windows I'd so far seen
were scratched and uneven.
The mist from our desire clouds what we look at.

Mountain Village

A frighteningly beautiful sunset
made the window panes glow
and the milk churns glitter
in a mountain village in Austria,
seen from the train.
No doubt the alpine cows up there
the sheep and the goats up there
the faithful dogs up there
had nightly dreams up there
of plunging down vertical cliffs
and ten metres from tragedy
turning into swallows.

The Horsewoman

Someone is approaching in the dream whirls
far out on the campagna.
Man or woman?
A horsewoman!
Black-clad?
Black-clad, with red lining visible
when she suddenly wheels round.
Why does her horse shy?
Why does she turn?
For the sake of the snow-laden trees.
How do I know?
It's there to be read in Nordic sagas,
in poems written this year.

The Face

Here is a woman stooped forward combing her hair,
her very long chestnut-brown
crackling hair.

And here's a child sitting on the floor waiting
for the face hidden behind the crackling curtain
to be visible again.

The same eyes! The same nostrils! The same mouth!

The childish child cries.
The grown-up child swallows his cry.
The aged child mumbles.

The Painter

A widower, he could stand there on the gravel road
and with his gaze follow a cloud
until it died.
Of his wife's letters there remained
only scraps read through and through.
If he weren't hindered by canvasses he'd started on,
by brushes and complaining colours
he could have reconciled himself with the truth
of gravel roads, clouds and impossibilities.
(No-one can win!)
Was life a dream?
Yes, life was a dream, with hard outer edges.

Words without Song

In canoes no bigger than peapods
they broke the bounds of the known world
often singing.

On horses no bigger than dogs
they scaled 15,000 foot mountains
and gazed out over gardens
which at once were lauded in hymns.

Only with throats, tongues and lips
could statues be toppled and iron gates opened.

Then came the songless ironic period.
Half-eaten worms squirm in beaks.

The Translator

He had paid his electricity bills
for both winter and spring.
There now remained his debt to the sun.
One couldn't say it was dark
yet it was hardly light enough to start
a new version of Echnaton's hymn to the sun.
Then from Lake Immeln a three-master
arrived with a load of native sunbeams.
Brightness increased.
Orders streamed in from divers creatures
who wanted their cries interpreted.
The shining fish, including the bleak, demanded
to be written with their lustre intact.

He's Standing There Still, They Say

He stood there for ages, that man in an alley on Crete,
beating a small octopus against a stone wall
first to kill it
then to tenderize his tough supper.
Great changes have taken place in Europe,
a new flag raised.
Of the situation in Melancholia, a country without a flag,
I am better informed.
I usually ask returned travellers
if they've seen a man in a black beret
with a small octopus in his hand

before a stone wall.
Many have seen him.
He's standing there still,
they say.

The Driver

He picked me up on Södermalmstorg,
Self-drive hire, convertible with motorized top.
Just press a button.
I don't remember where we were going,
or if he had any purpose for the day.
How did he drive?
Sensitively, but not according to the law.
By passing a traffic island on the wrong side
he managed to steal half a second
from the owner of centuries and millennia.
On the crowded roads
he overtook everything in front of us.
With our three free hands we could have played poker.
Instead he pressed that button.
It wasn't raining,
nor was the sun intolerably bright.
Growling and groaning like a weight-lifter
a motor tried to lever up the black sail-cloth
that fluttered wildly and bulged in the airflow.
Firmly rooted trees witnessed our progress.
However old and experienced the old oaks may be
they'll never understand a human's laughter
when something goes to pieces and flies off in rags.

The Bird

No-one asks for the phoenix any more
though it's beautiful and finely glazed
and comes in three sizes.
Each morning they carry their birds
down the steep steps to the harbour
and hope some boat with buyers
and tourists from the mainland
will put in as they used to.

None,
however eagerly they wave.

There's no lack of skilled craftsmen.
They could well produce firearms,
bullet-proof waistcoats, pin-ball machines
and other items the market's crying out for.

In the meantime they carry on copying,
firing and gilding the phoenix,
the bird that will rise from the ashes.

Elegy

She grounds the mountains to gravel in her mill
and the gravel to sand in her mortar,
she who transforms everything.

For the humans in the intertwined years
it was the softest of beds,
the one between stone-pines and ocean.
Lizards, plovers and beetles
told us they existed,
had existed.

For she who transforms everything
doesn't want the kingdom of sand to last either.
Between her fingers she rubs it down to dust
for the wind to spread.

Almost without bodies, with volatile souls,
sitting on two kitchen chairs
we've brought from the world of the senses,
we try to recall the colours.
How many were there, besides sand-yellow?
Three.
Sky-blue. Grass-green.
And the one that bleeds.

In the Sand Box

I sit here among creatures called children
and pour sand into their buckets.

They turn their filled buckets upsides down
and eagerly shout: 'Look! Look!'

then receive due praise for their towers of sand
— which they promptly annihilate

and pedal off on their tricycles
to the swings and climbing frames

and I'm left on my own with last night's vision:
Fire, not water, ran in all the rivers.

(Outside the fence trams clatter past
with perishable creatures in them.)

Fire, not water, ran in all the rivers
and flowed into a gold-foil-glittering sea.

But out of that motionless beauty islands rose,
treeless, bloody, like flayed animal bodies.

The small savages, a touch older now but still children,
climb down from the frames and ask for more sand.

I help them to build new towers of sand.
They help me to forget the night's dream.

(And all the time trams clatter past
with perishable creatures in them.)

Pain

The fare on the good ship PAIN leaves nothing to grumble about:
black and white tablets, lemon-yellow and carrot-red pills,
merciful drinks in small plastic beakers.
Extra doses at night.
Those who still can't sleep are gathered on deck
to howl at the moon or the on-duty planet.
Others stay in their cabins, curl up like embryos
and whisper to themselves: 'You're not here ...
you're not here ... you're not ...'
A man parks his torment outside the Altamira Cave
and goes in to the bisons and the horses
that have galloped round the walls for twenty thousand years.
A woman walked with her grandmother on the trembling bridge
over the wild water-race in Uppsala, past the pastry shop
to the cathedral, where Christ and the magpies lived.

The medicine trolley disappears, rattling down the corridor.
The beautiful hour is near
when the sense of proportion fades out.
The girl in the neighbour's garden was stooped over her zither.

I crept up and undid her hair-band
so that her locks tumbled over her face, her zither and the table.
This resounding tent of first love
was higher than Everest, Mount Blanc, Kilimanjaro,
Städjan and other peaks listed in the geography book.
But the good ship PAIN steams ahead.
The ship refuses to sink.
S.O.S.

Longing

The new moon is mirrored in earth's puddles.
A night nurse leans over a bed
to jab into place a pillow for someone old
who is going to die next day.
How helpful and healthy the Finnish girls are.
A feeble arm reaches up to the beautiful arm,
the unreachable, the girl from Karelia.
There is a worn word for this distance
between hand and cheek
and the eye's memory of an astrakhan high up.

Infinity and the Loaf of Bread

Bed-ridden, tethered by two tubes,
I try to imagine infinity.
I lift off the hospital roof
as the astronomer at night opens the observatory dome.
Eternity has not changed much
since it was last in my thoughts:
white-haired, no wrinkles, neither man nor woman.
Far out on the icy expanse of infinity
the astronomer sees someone approaching.
It's his wife, she's breathing calmly.
What she has in her hand is breathing too,
a loaf of bread, newly baked, with currants in it.

(In hospital, 28:04:96)

Dear Squirrel

'He who sits in the shade of his own tail.'
You know I once praised you in some clumsy lines.
Now I'd like a favour of you, a loan.
As guarantee I can offer you a hazel bush,
taller and more wide-reaching than Yggdrasil.
With my wife I was sitting on a bench
by Lake Klara.
Silently on that water not made by man
there glided a pale blue man-made canoe.

The man in it rests his paddle and allows his boat
to edge forward to the sluice-gate
where it turns into an aircraft
and rises above the City Hall, the Palace, the whole
                                                    metropolis,
away towards the enormous hazel bush, where you
could potter about gathering nuts for winter.
For the winters won't stop.
May I borrow your tail for a day or two
to shade myself from the dark?

Dear squirrel?